ENTERPRISE MOBILITY
BREAKTHROUGH

ENTERPRISE MOBILITY
BREAKTHROUGH

THE BEGINNERS GUIDE

RAGHVENDRA SINGH DIKHIT

Foreword by Aditya Saxena

PARTRIDGE
A Penguin Random House Company

Print information available on the last page.

To order additional copies of this book, contact
Partridge India
000 800 10062 62
orders.india@partridgepublishing.com

www.partridgepublishing.com/india

IN LOVING MEMORY OF

PROF. (DR.) ASHWANI KUMAR RAMANI

SCHOOL OF COMPUTER SCIENCE, DAVV, INDORE (MP), INDIA.

Contents

Foreword

Raghvendra is my colleague, we worked together on many enterprise mobility solutions, and we always felt the absence of an introductory book on enterprise mobility. I am glad to see this book from him. This book touches all aspects of enterprise mobility solutions and offers fair details for each of them. It is a good starting point for all curious minds who would like to understand enterprise mobility.

Generally mobility used to be considered a small part of the entire solution offered, but after going through this book, you will realize that it is a separate discipline that demands significant investments in terms of time, money, and energy.

Enterprise mobility is a fusion of technologies. It is difficult to put all information in logical flow, but the author (Raghvendra) has designed all chapters thoughtfully. Each chapter starts with key points and ends with a summary. I am sure this arrangement will help readers in consolidating their thoughts, and they will be able to map their understanding with the author's viewpoint.

Happy reading!

Aditya Saxena
Enterprise Mobility Leader

Preface

Thing that one has is not big. Else everything is the big thing.

Enterprise mobility is emerging and proliferating. It's a buzzword and topic for debate, but if one would ask 'What is enterprise mobility?' then there might be a pause or may be a speech with several examples and use cases. Information or data is available from assorted sources, but in a very scattered manner. If one would like to consult something consolidated to understand enterprise mobility, then it is missing, at least for beginners. The reasons foreseen are emerging trends of enterprise mobility with time, hence, introducing new concepts and integrating them. It demands to cope with new technology, hardware, and their collaboration with software to serve enterprise-specific needs.

One of the challenges that are faced is that a lot of content is available for marketing and sales by versatile vendors, manufacturers, service providers, and companies. Thus, they provide information and content with marketing and sales perspective. Hence, an independent view for understanding and learning is missing.

This book is a breakthrough for beginners and intermediates of enterprise mobility. Scholars, executives, and experts can major on the scale and scope of enterprise mobility athirst for knowledge. This book focuses upon basic concepts and details and features mobile applications and popular technical and marketing phrases. The content is independent of any specific product, service, or solution by any particular company.

This book is an independent view on enterprise mobility, which is beneficial to business heads, technical architects, project managers, analysts, system administrators, project leads, and developers for enterprise mobility design, development, support, and maintenance.

This book has been classified in seven sections.

Section 1 introduces enterprise mobility with definition, objective, focus areas, needs, and challenges of enterprises, also detailing the evolution of enterprise mobility with history overview.

Section 2 details enterprise mobility ecosystem, landscape, and maturity model. Enterprise mobility maturity model defines levels as per enterprise adaption of mobile strategy, solution, and management. Enterprise mobility ecosystem and landscape highlights participating factors and systems. This particular section is important to understand the analogy behind enterprise mobility.

Enterprise mobility is surrounded with technical acronyms and terminologies (EMM, EAS, MAM, MDM, MCM, and MEM). Section 3 provides concept and detail of EMM (enterprise mobility management). And it incorporates overview of EMM components.

Solutions are incomplete without technology. Section 4 emphasizes on technology with focus on mobile solutions. This section describes leading mobile platforms, form factors, and types of mobile applications.

Section 5 traverses through enterprise mobile application information flow, architecture, layered structure, and other components. It inspects popular and important architecture ingredients (push notification, SSO, mBaaS, SOA, and MEAP).

There are trends other than technology which influence enterprise mobility. These trends are either design philosophy, user psychology, or marketing phrase. Section 6 shares paradigms of mobile first, gamification, IOT, and hybrid.

Lastly, section 7 is a case study for an enterprise mobile solution with defined needs and challenges. It incorporates solution overview, use cases, architecture, and system flow.

Summary points, recommended best practices, and other enterprise mobility thoughts are covered on appendix sections.

I wish you an informative and knowledgeable reading!

Acknowledgements

This book is based on my understanding and experience on enterprise mobility. I am grateful for a number of colleagues, mentors, and supervisors for supporting and encouraging me to work on enterprise mobility.

My sincere gratitude to Aditya Saxena, my mentor and colleague, for his support, guidance, and mentorship. He encouraged and helped me to write the book.

I am thankful to Amitabh Srivastava for providing me the opportunities to work on enterprise mobility projects, products, and solutions.

I would like to acknowledge D Saiprabhu Rao, more a friend than colleague, for conceptualizing and designing the cover page of the book.

I would like to share a special note of thanks to Sujata Ramani, Chhavi Gangwal, and Khushaboo Ramani for their help and support on the book review.

Finally, I am very thankful to God for such a supportive family, especially for my mother (Chetan Dikhit) and father (Rajkumar Singh Dikhit), for their moral support and motivation. Last but not the least, I am grateful to my wife (Vandana Dikhit) and son (Raajas Dikhit) for sparing and allowing me to work on this book.

Thank you all!

List of Figures

Definitions, Acronyms, and Abbreviations

AngularJS:	Open-source web application framework
Apache Cordova:	Platform for building mobile applications using HTML, CSS, and JS
API:	Application programming interfaces
APNS:	Apple Push Notification service
Arduino:	It is a group of single-board microcontrollers to build interactive objects
ASM:	Area service manager
B2B:	Business-to-business
B2C:	Business-to-consumer
B2E:	Business-to-employee
BaaS:	Backend as a Service
BB:	BlackBerry
BBM:	BlackBerry messenger
BES:	BlackBerry enterprise server
BI:	Business intelligence
BIS:	BlackBerry Internet service
Bootstrap:	It is HTML-, CSS-, and JS-based framework for developing responsive mobile and web applications
BYOA:	Bring your own application
BYOD:	Bring your own device
C2DM:	Cloud-to-device messaging
CCXML:	Call control extensible markup language
CIO:	Chief information officer
CMS:	Content management system
CoAP:	Constrained application protocol

Cocoa:	Apple's native object-oriented application programming interface
COPE:	Corporate-owned personally enabled
CRM:	Customer relationship management
CRUD:	Create, read, update, delete
CSS:	Cascading style sheets
CYOD:	Choose your own device
DTMF:	Dual-tone multifrequency signalling
EAI:	Enterprise application integration
EAM:	Enterprise architecture management
EAM:	Enterprise asset management
EAS:	Enterprise app store
ECM:	Enterprise content management
EI:	Enterprise integration
EII:	Enterprise information integration
EIM:	Enterprise information management
EM:	Enterprise mobility
Embedded System:	A computer system based on microcontrollers for dedicated function within a larger system
EMM:	Enterprise mobility management
EMM:	Enterprise marketing management
ERP:	Enterprise resource planning
ESP:	Enterprise social platforms
ESS:	Enterprise social software
FAQ:	Frequently asked questions
FOTA:	Firmware over-the-air
FSE:	Field service engineer
FSM:	Field service management
GCM:	Google Cloud Messaging
GPS:	Global Positioning System
GRXML:	Grammar extensible markup language (aka speech recognition grammar specification)
GSM:	Global System for Mobile communications

HCM:	Human capital management
HRIS:	Human resource information system
HRMS:	Human resource management system
HTML:	Hypertext markup language
HTTP:	Hypertext transfer protocol
HTTPS:	Hypertext transfer protocol secure
IDE:	Integrated development environment
IM:	Instant messaging
iOS:	Mobile operating system by Apple (previously iPhone OS)
IOT:	Internet of things
ISV:	Independent software vendor
IT:	Information technology
IVR:	Interactive voice response
Java EE:	Java platform enterprise edition
JS:	JavaScript
jQuery:	JavaScript library which provides fast and feature-rich support for HTML-, CSS-, and JS-based application implementation
jQuery Mobile:	It is a touch-optimized JavaScript framework for mobile applications
LBS:	Location-based services
LDAP:	Lightweight directory access protocol
LESS:	It is CSS preprocessor which extends CSS language. It provides versatile features like allow variables, mixins, functions, etc. to make CSS maintainable, theme-able, and extendable
MAM:	Mobile application management
mBaaS:	Mobile Backend as a Service
MCM:	Mobile content management
MDM:	Mobile device management
MEAP:	Mobile enterprise application platform
MEM:	Mobile expense management
MQTT:	Message queuing telemetry transport

MVC:	Model view controller
MVP:	Minimum viable product
MVVM:	Model-View-ViewModel
NDK:	Native development kit
NFC:	Near field communication
OCR:	Optical character recognition
OEM:	Original equipment manufacturer
OS:	Operating system
OTA:	Over-the-air
PBL:	Points, badges, and leaderboards
PCL:	Portable class library
PDA:	Personal digital assistant
PushSharp:	Open-source third-party server side library for push notification support on diverse platforms
Raspberry Pi:	Small size single-board computer
REST:	Representational State Transfer (RESTful)
RFID:	Radio frequency identification
RIM:	Research in Motion
RMS:	Records management system
ROI:	Return on investment
RTP:	Real-time transport protocol
RTSP:	Real-time streaming protocol
SAAS:	Software as a Service
SCM:	Supply chain management
SCS:	Social collaboration software
SDK:	Software development kit
SEP:	Social enterprise platform
SI:	Systems integrator
Smart Object:	An object with own possible interactions
SMB:	Small medium-sized business
SME:	Subject matter expert
SMEs:	Small medium-sized enterprises
SMM:	Social media management
SMS:	Short Message Service

SOA:	Service-oriented architecture
SOAP:	Simple object access protocol
SPI:	Serial peripheral interface
SRF:	Shaped radio frequency signal
SSO:	Single sign-on
Symbian:	A mobile operating system for smartphones
TCO:	Total cost of ownership
TCP:	Transmission control protocol
UART:	Universal asynchronous receiver transmitter
UDP:	User datagram protocol
UPN:	Unified Push Notification
UI:	User interface
UX:	User experience
VoIP:	Voice over Internet Protocol
VPN:	Virtual private network
VXML:	Voice extensible markup language
Wi-Fi:	wireless fidelity
WMN:	Wireless mesh network
WNS:	Windows Push Notification Service
WP:	Windows Phone
WP8:	Widows Phone 8
WPF:	Windows Presentation Foundation

1. INTRODUCTION

KEY POINTS COVERED

- ❖   Enterprise Mobility Definition
- ❖   Heterogeneous Application Types
- ❖   Major Mobile History Facts
- ❖   Enterprise Mobility Stages
- ❖   Enterprise Mobility Objective

Enterprise mobility has a long way to go with unexplored and untapped areas. And its market is too big to ignore. Ubiquitous mobile and Internet usage have transported enterprise mobility towards an ocean of opportunities. A massive growth has been observed in the sale of smartphones and tablets. With capabilities besides quad-core processors, decent memory, and bigger screen size, smart devices are ideal for personal and professional use. Gadgets owned by the target user—employees, partners, distributors, contractors, and customers—are smarter than the technology options provided by the enterprises, which is a huge challenge for the enterprises. Organizations are trying hard to come up with an efficient, secure, and usable catalyst across multiple platforms to meet the expectations and demands of the target users.

1.1 Enterprise Mobility

Mobile applications have changed the focus from what's on the web to the applications on mobile device. Mobile apps are no longer an option; they are now an imperative, even a measurable ROI (return on investment) for enterprises. Many factors play a crucial role in enterprise mobile strategy—namely, device management, online/offline behaviour, timely upgrade, data security, extensibility, scalability, and multiplatform supported application. An enterprise's objective to consider all these factors while finalizing a strategy and execution is all about *enterprise mobility*.

Note

Enterprise mobility is a term applied for complete range of mobile solutions, designed for business to be used by enterprise users (partners, customers, distributors, contractors, and employees).
• •

Needlessly, it can be said that all the solutions working within an enterprise which possesses a mobile component comes under enterprise mobility. Thus, all the VoIP solutions (hardware and software), mobile data and voice plans, mobile applications, etc. would also be a part of enterprise mobility, where the majority of chunks of mobile applications are developed to serve enterprise objectives at distinctive business levels.

1.1.1 Mobile App Classification

Mobile applications under the umbrella of enterprise mobility can be classified as per solution or business essential. Applications can also be categorized on the basis of target users or segments with different business perspectives. Following are the application categories:

[I.]   B2B (Business-to-business): This kind of application possesses a channel of communication between business to business, with embracing respective information flows and commercial aspects of enterprises. For example an application for a manufacturer and dealer featuring transactions, interactions, records, orders, etc.

[II.]   B2C (Business-to-consumer): These applications are targeted for the consumer segment. There can be a wide variety of consumer-oriented applications. For example a catalogue application of enterprise products and services for end consumers.

[III.]   B2E (Business-to-employee): Here the target segment or users are the enterprise employees. Such applications are intended for employee productivity and efficiency. For example a leave management mobile application of enterprise for employees.

[IV.]   Enterprise Mobile Applications: These mobile applications are designed and implemented as per enterprise need. They are intended to serve enterprise objectives of mobile client application for communication and collaboration by authorized enterprise users.

[V.]   Composite Mobile Applications: Applications which are a part of a system or portion of a solution. Basically they are pieces of software applications. For example, application on leave management system of ERP (enterprise resource planning) would be a composite mobile application.

[VI.]   Vertical Mobile Applications: These mobile applications target well-defined classified business objectives. And they are used by determined users. Such applications are designed and developed for desired business objectives as per user skill set. This may require customization to integrate with other business process or flow. For example a mobile application designed for an enterprise sales team to promote the product and service would be a vertical mobile application.

[VII.]   Horizontal Mobile Applications: These applications are off-the-shelf catalyst solutions designed and developed to work with diversified industries. These applications are not targeted for specific industries or domains but can be customized and deployed easily for any enterprise. For example off-the-shelf application on customer care is a horizontal mobile application where it is implemented to cover customer needs and respective workflows. As per requirement, this application can be customized and deployed for any enterprise.

An enterprise mobile application can be owned by multiple categories. For example there can be a B2B vertical enterprise mobile application.

1.2 Needs and Challenges

Enterprises stress at gaining competitive advantage. User delight, efficient/productive workforce, and resource optimization lead them to versatile challenges for mobility solutions. They can be like:

[I.]   Data Security: Mobility solution requires enterprise data access. And in cases, application saves enterprise data locally at user's personal device. Security mechanism for data on the move as well as data-at-rest is one of the crucial concerns for enterprises.

   o   Data on the move: Data security while network communication for client–server interaction

   o   Data at rest: Data security while storage at mobile device (required for offline data support from mobile application)

[II.]   Enterprise Data Gateway: Access of enterprise data over generic Wi-Fi or operator's network is a core requirement of modern mobility solutions. These gateways should have intelligence to offer enterprise data at registered devices only. However, these data sources may be standard or custom data sources.

[III.]   Device/Platform Diversity: Multiplatform supported applications for supporting BYOD (bring your own device) or CYOD (choose your own device) policy are an unavoidable need for enterprises. COPE (corporate-owned personally enabled) devices might also be a mode of delivery. Selection of appropriate development strategy to deal with platform diversity and device diversity is one of the important decisions. It can significantly affect TCO (total cost of ownership). Applications in in-house distribution and admin desk to manage user devices in remote fashion also add to TCO.

[IV.]   Manageability (application distribution and data management): Data management and applications management in a remote manner is another expensive dimension of enterprise mobility ecosystem.

[V.]   User Experience: Customer/user delight is the way to engage them with offerings/services. Mobile solutions come with diverse platform-specific guidelines and user interaction models like Windows Metro guidelines, iOS (mobile operating system by Apple) human interface guidelines, Android UX guidelines, etc. Mobile applications can be designed with app-centric design or adaptive design.

- o App-centric design: Mobile application designed with common guidelines and used across the multiple platform devices.
- o Adaptive design: Mobile applications designed with respective platform-specific guidelines for desired cross platforms.

Considering the difficulties and challenges with mobile strategies, enterprises are looking for a unique and cost-effective catalyst solution that reduces the time to arrive at market and offers high maintainability.

1.3 Enterprise Mobility Evolution

Enterprise solutions emerge over time as per the transfers introduced via society, technology, revolution, or invention. The mobile is one of such gadgets which postulate enterprises to look over on their solution offerings. With time, enterprises are looking forward for mobile strategies and future aspects. Needlessly, the cause is very simple because mobile grades virally in the society.

1.3.1 History

If we go to history for mobile devices and mobile technologies, then 1985 to 2000 was the time for the PDA (personal digital assistant). By 2003 onwards, BlackBerry devices captured the market for professional use, and Nokia with Symbian OS was leading for personal mobile devices. The years 2007 to 2008 were the time of revolution in mobile history with iOS and Android release. BlackBerry was leading the market for professional use till the time the iPhone and Android were released, though the iPhone and Android smartphone were not basically intended only for professional use. Later on, people started to use two phones—one for business and the other for personal use. Latest handheld devices harness robust hardware configurations and processing capabilities to manage personal and professional work with one device. Below are the years of revolution in mobile history:

[I.]   1984: First PDA (personal digital assistant) was released by Psion.

[II.]   1992: First GSM (Global System for Mobile communications) phone Nokia 1011 had been introduced.

[III.] 1994: IBM introduced first PDA with mobile phone functionality.

[IV.]   1996: Nokia introduced 9000 Communicator PDA with mobile phone functionality, which became the world's best-selling PDA.

[V.]   1997: Symbian mobile operating system was released by EPOC32.

[VI.]   1999: First BlackBerry 850 device released, a two-way email pager.

[VII.] 2000: HP introduced Windows-based iPAQ device.

[VIII.] 2002: Symbian S60 platform had been launched. This led fame and major market share to Nokia devices.

[IX.]   2003: Convergent smartphone BlackBerry had been released with push email, text messaging, mobile telephone, web browser, and other wireless services.

[X.]   2007: First iOS (Apple operating system) had been launched with iPhone.

[XI.]   2008: First commercial release of Android operating system.

[XII.] 2010: iPad (tablet computer) based on iOS had been launched by Apple.

[XIII.] 2012: Windows Phone 8 had been released by Microsoft.

[XIV.] 2013: New operating system BlackBerry 10 had been released.

[XV.]   2014: Apple had introduced iOS 8, and Android Lollipop 5.0 had been released.

1.3.2 Evolution

Over a period, versatile technologies have emerged. However, irrespective of emerging technology or market trend, enterprises possess their own needs and challenges. They are data security, manageability, scalability, reliability, development/support cost, user experience, cross-platform support, etc. with enterprises. The chief focus areas are as follows:

[I.]   gain competitive advantage
[II.]   user delight
[III.] efficient/productive workforce
[IV.]   resource optimization.

In order to break through challenges and fulfil the need of desired focus areas, enterprise solutions have also emerged with time. The mobile, as a mandatory gadget for users, has given a new direction to enterprise solutions. Mobile-centric solutions and services have emerged as an essential for enterprises due to target user dependency on mobiles. People are willing to access everything from their mobiles, either for personal or professional use. It is also an untapped opportunity for business.

Note

Objective for enterprise mobility can be defined as:

Enhancements in productivity with measurable ROI using mobility strategies, solutions, and management for enterprise users, and business flows are the principal focus of enterprise mobility.

1.3.2.1 EM Stages

Enterprises would require mobile-centric services, consulting, and respective solutions from SMEs (subject matter experts). Broadly enterprise mobility can be classified in three stages.

[I.]   Mobility Strategies: Well-defined enterprise policies are required for identification of any strategy. Enterprise policies are important in view of security and management perspective. Also, it gives direction for solutions design and their offerings. Mobile offering is a part of overall enterprise strategies, which is required to be identified and well defined before planning further actions. These strategies are the enablers for transforming enterprises to exploit market business opportunities. Mobile strategies would drive the path for enterprise mobility.

[II.]   Mobility Solutions: Enterprises would necessitate different catalysts as per business flow and execution cycle. These catalysts may or may not possess mobile offerings. However, in today's era, it is unavoidable to plan solutions without mobile perspectives. Enterprise mobility focuses on mobility roots for the containment of mobile products, solutions, and services.

[III.] Mobility Management: Designed and implemented solutions management emphasizes on certain aspects. They are infrastructure requirement, their setup, processes and resources for execution, etc. Mobiles can be one of the causes for security menace which requires concentrated approaches and catalysts to maintain enterprise data secure and manageable.

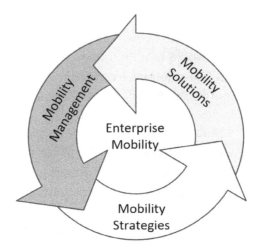

Figure 1-1: EM Stages

The diagram illustrates the three distinctive stages of enterprise mobility in circular direction. These three classified stages work in a circular way in enterprise while execution. Strategies are built over time. They get mature with end-user feedbacks, results, and business-oriented reports. Solutions are also updated over the period with versatile innovations, emerging technologies, and market trends. Management features and support are the outcome of emerging and evolving essentials from strategies and solutions.

SUMMING UP

✓   Enterprise mobility is a term applied for complete range of mobile solutions designed for businesses, to be used by enterprise users (partners, customers, distributors, contractors, and employees).

✓   All the solutions working at enterprises which harness mobile components come under enterprise mobility.

✓   Solution-oriented apps
   ➢ Enterprise mobile applications
   ➢ Composite mobile applications
   ➢ Vertical mobile applications
   ➢ Horizontal mobile applications

- ✓ Business-oriented apps
  - ➢ Business-to-business
  - ➢ Business-to-consumer
  - ➢ Business-to-employee
- ✓ Enterprise needs and challenges
  - ➢ Data security
  - ➢ Enterprise data gateway
  - ➢ Device/platform diversity
  - ➢ Manageability
  - ➢ User experience
- ✓ Enterprise focus areas
  - ➢ Gain competitive advantage
  - ➢ User delight
  - ➢ Efficient/productive workforce
  - ➢ Resource optimization
- ✓ Enterprise mobility stages
  - ➢ Mobility strategies
  - ➢ Mobility solutions
  - ➢ Mobility management
- ✓ Enterprise mobility objective: Enhancements in productivity with measurable ROI using mobility strategies and solutions. And management for enterprise users and business flows is the principal focus of enterprise mobility.

ACTION ITEMS

- ✓ What are the Gartner predictions for enterprise mobility?
- ✓ List down the leading VoIP solution providers.
- ✓ List down the differences among vertical versus horizontal solutions.
- ✓ Is enterprise mobility a major concern for CIOs?
- ✓ Identify the reasons from enterprises for avoiding mobile solutions.
- ✓ List down the benefits which enterprises can leverage with mobile solutions.

2. MATURITY MODEL

KEY POINTS COVERED

- ❖ EM Ecosystem
- ❖ EM Landscape—Needs and Enablers
- ❖ Enterprise Systems (FSM, CRM, SCP, ERP, ESP, ECM)
- ❖ EM Maturity Model

An enterprise has many business departments, employees, and stakeholders.

[I.]   Business Departments: Marketing, sales, finance, human resource, inventory, payroll, transportation, administration, etc.

[II.]   Employees: Executives, managers, SMEs (subject matter experts), workers/engineers/labourers, etc.

[III.] Stakeholders: Investors, partners, distributors, vendors, OEMs (original equipment manufacturers), ISVs (independent software vendors), SI (systems integrators), etc.

An enterprise can be of small, mid, or large size. Earlier, only large enterprises were considered to embrace well-defined catalysts in their execution cycle, due to cost and infrastructure overheads. However, over time, thought process and enterprise objectives have been evolved, and now business software systems are also used by SMEs (small medium-sized enterprises), though the primary reasons might be a competition, customer satisfaction, popularity of smart devices, or cost-effective technology. Mobility offerings as a part of business roots have given innovative direction for effective and efficient execution at an enterprise's workplace.

2.1 Enterprise Mobility Ecosystem

Enterprise mobility ecosystem (EM ecosystem) is an aura of the enterprise in the light of mobiles. It helps to identify the surrounding entities and atmosphere actors for mobile insights. Knowledge of the EM ecosystem is the first step for reckoning of any mobile solution.

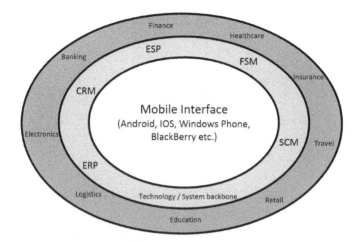

Figure 2-1: EM Ecosystem

Three broad levels of classification for EM ecosystem are as follows:

[I.]   Enterprise Domain: Outer ellipse of the diagram represents the enterprise domain. It plays an important role for any software solution. Each domain possesses their own challenges, demands, and key ingredients. Solutions designs, offerings, and features should be aligned with the needs and challenges of the domain. It's feasible to leverage ready-to-deploy-and-use domain-specific solutions, services, and products offered by different vendors.

[II.]   Business Core System: Middle ellipse of the diagram is for enterprise core systems, business units, and technology backbones. This is the building block to fabricate any mobile solution or application at the enterprise.

[III.] Mobile Interface: Inner ellipse of the diagram is for mobile interface. It is the final outcome of solution, which is used by desired users though it is required to process a complete cycle of execution to construct a mobile interface. These mobile applications can be on diverse popular devices and platforms (Android, iOS, WP, or BlackBerry) as per enterprise user's device environment.

2.2 Enterprise Mobility Landscape

Enterprise mobility landscape shows paradigms in EM ecosystem. It considers all the generic widely used components and entities.

Broadly it can be classified as *needs* and *enablers*. *Needs* are those entities which are required to be considered while designing enterprise mobility solutions. And *enablers* are additional enhancements or catalysts for mobility solutions.

Enablers – Tools, technology & frameworks		
Cross platform mobile app development tool	EMM	Mobile data protection/ security tools
	MDM/MAM	
Sync platforms		Push notification
	EAS	gateways
Mobile test automation tools		
	MEAP	Purpose built devices

Needs – Mobile extension of enterprise systems						
ERP	CRM	SCM	ESP	ECM	FSM	...

Figure 2-2: EM Landscape

Enterprise mobility landscape can be classified as:

[I.]   Needs: These are the mobile extension of enterprise systems, which are an imperative foundation of enterprise mobility solutions.

o ERP (enterprise resource planning)

o   CRM (customer relationship management)
o   SCM (supply chain management)
o   FSM (field service management)
o   ESP (enterprise social platform)
o   ECM (enterprise content management)
o   BI (business intelligence) tools, etc.

[II.]   Enablers: These are versatile tools, technologies, and frameworks which are used as enablers or catalysts to build enterprise mobility solutions.
o   EMM (enterprise mobility management)
o   Cross-platform mobile app development tool
o   MEAP (mobile enterprise application platform)
o   Sync platforms
o   Mobile test automation tools
o   MDM (mobile device management)/MAM (mobile application management)
o   EAS (enterprise app store)
o   Push notification gateways
o   Purpose-built devices
o   Mobile data protection/security tools

2.2.1 Enterprise Systems

An enterprise has several business units and systems at execution level. Below are some of the popular acronyms used for enterprise segments or systems. It's difficult to exist in isolation for any system at enterprise. Hence, it is very obvious to embrace some overlap of features, solutions, and services within the system. Here, mobile perspective is emphasized more for each enterprise system under the halo of enterprise mobility.

2.2.1.1 Field Service Management (FSM)

Field service jobs are the area of complexity for enterprise as well as individuals. Field service schedule management, client interaction, and real-time task management are hectic and demanding. Field service life cycle can be defined as:

[I.]   new appointment
[II.]   assign resource
[III.]   process/execute with resource tracking
[IV.]   review/assess/feedback
[V.]   close/complete flow
[VI.]   analytics/reports.

Mobile-centric transformational solutions lead to an effective solution with better utilization of time and money for enterprises as well as individuals.

Field service management (FSM) is the solution or catalyst to entertain objectives of workforce optimizations for any enterprise. FSM solutions can affirm introductory features as:

[I.]   workforce management
[II.]   schedule management
[III.]   support data on the move (online/offline)
[IV.]   real-time statistics
[V.]   location tracking
[VI.]   business intelligence
[VII.]   social network collaboration
[VIII.]   payment gateway integration.

Mobiles can be facilitators for data collection, user feedback, schedule, etc., as per desired FSM solution. These solutions inherit benefits likewise increased efficiency, time-based routing, real-time analysis, and optimized cost/time.

2.2.1.2 Customer Relationship Management (CRM)

One of the imperative needs for any enterprise is an efficient CRM. It is the system for enterprise customers' management. The CRM system plays an important role to feed enterprise core motives. Basic objectives behind CRM systems are customer acquisition, retention, and migration with increased profitability. It primarily deals with sales, marketing, and the customer which are important entities for any business.

The CRM solution possesses the following features but aren't limit to:

[I.]   contact and account management
[II.]   communication tracking
[III.] scheduling
[IV.]   sales automation, tracking, and forecasting
[V.]   marketing automation
[VI.]   customer service
[VII.] knowledge management.

Customer engagement can be defined in three steps as below.

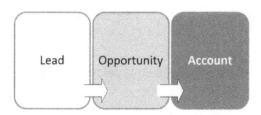

Figure 2-3: CRM Engagement Steps

Here, *lead* is a new identified person or company that can have potential to be an opportunity. *Opportunity* is the potential lead. It goes through versatile sales stages (proposal, quote, etc.) for selling a product or service. *Account* is engaged lead with business relationships though it's not necessary to initiate purchase of any service or product yet.

2.2.1.3 Supply Chain Management (SCM)

Enterprises manufacturing systems require solutions to deal with end-to-end cycles from supplier to consumer. SCM (supply chain management) is all about managing the life cycle from supplier to consumer as per enterprise need. Goods supplier, product manufacturing, warehouses, transportation/distribution, and customers are the entities/parties involved with any supply chain management system. SCM has introduced versatile changes and innovations from time to time as per emerging technologies. Mobiles had introduced respectively optimized and innovative solutions to the SCM ecosystem. Even mobile offerings had become an essential for the SCM system of any enterprise.

The following are some of the features offered by SCM but are not limited to:

[I.]   inventory management
[II.]   worker management
[III.]   controlling and tracking data, flow, and locations
[IV.]   real-time schedule, notifications, and alerts
[V.]   real-time information at different levels
[VI.]   logistics and reports.

Innovative SCM system provides reduced employee downtime, responsiveness to customers, control, and tracking of overall system. Mobile apps with location, map, and adequate information help to optimize frequently changing time-critical supply chain ecosystem.

2.2.1.4 Enterprise Resource Planning (ERP)

ERP is an acronym for enterprise resource planning which focuses on enterprise business process integration, automation, and management. It can be used by small, mid, or large enterprises, though earlier it was implied to be used by mid or large enterprises only due to cost overheads. The ERP system is comprised of several modules also known as ERP modules, and each module can sustain separate solutions or software for particular purposes, like payroll.

The following are some of the imperative features of ERP but are not limited to:

[I.]   manage project planning, cost, and development

[II.]   payroll, account, and finance process automation

[III.]   data protection via well-defined role-based data access

[IV.]   document management

[V.]   workflow management

[VI.]   employee life cycle management

[VII.]   manufacturing process automation

[VIII.]   human resource process automation

[IX.]   sales and marketing process management

[X.]   collaboration management

[XI.]   messaging/chat support

[XII.]   inventory and procurement management

[XIII.]   reports and performance monitoring for optimizations.

It is very common to compare ERP with CRM due to overlap of assorted features. However, broadly CRM deals with front office management (sales, marketing, business contacts/profiles, accounts, etc.), whereas ERP focuses on back office business process integrations (payroll, account, finance, employee management, workflow management, project management, etc.) though some systems integrate both CRM and ERP to prevent data isolation.

ERP systems help enterprises to improve operation efficiency, integrate all business processes, and manage back-office activities.

2.2.1.5 Enterprise Social Platform (ESP)

ESP is an acronym for enterprise social platform, which is one of the must-have solutions for enterprises with a principal focus on collaboration, communication, and coordination among different business units and members. The ESP system needs secure and robust system with a portal. It can hold topic, activity stream, or group-oriented subcommunities. And there can be internal as well as external platforms for engagement in the enterprise's social community.

ESP focuses on management of the following features but aren't limit to:

[I.]   wiki, forums, calendar, polls, messenger
[II.]   unified search, collaboration, FAQs
[III.]   documents, email notifications
[IV.]   product or service promotion
[V.]   user profile, connections, localization
[VI.]   web content management.

ESS (enterprise social software) is also a coined acronym in the enterprise ecosystem. It also focuses on enhancing communication, collaboration, and coordination among business units, employees, and processes. There are some other acronyms which are in use with similar features, like SEP (social enterprise platform) and SCS (social collaboration software).

2.2.1.6 Enterprise Content Management (ECM)

Enterprise content management (ECM) is a combination of methods, strategies, and tools, with systematic ways to capture, store, manage, preserve, and access information, content, and documents related to the enterprise. It governs the life cycle of information, from its creation to publication through archives and later on its disposal.

The ECM system includes the following features but aren't limit to:

[I.]   document management
[II.]   web content management
[III.]   records management
[IV.]   digital asset management

[V.]   workflow/process management
[VI.]   security, search, localization
[VII.]   archive, backup, and recovery management
[VIII.]   version control.

EIM (enterprise information management) is one of the acronyms used in the enterprise ecosystem for similar kinds of features.

2.3 Enterprise Mobility Maturity Model

Enterprise mobility maturity model defines levels of enterprise maturity over mobility. There are assorted parameters which drive mobile awareness, enablement, or engagement at enterprise:

[I.]   industry-specific business analysis and growth parameters
[II.]   enterprise needs, expectations, and mobile strategies
[III.]   end-to-end ecosystem design
[IV.]   infrastructure required
[V.]   feasibility, scalability, maintainability, operability for desired solution
[VI.]   technology stack and constraints
[VII.]   app designs, UX and usability, users behaviour
[VIII.]   app development, testing, distribution
[IX.]   problem-driven R & D
[X.]   overall solution cost
[XI.]   feedback, analysis, reports, and charts.

Enterprises can be categorized on the basis of their mobile solution readiness. An enterprise may target transformation to higher levels in the maturity model.

There are three levels in the enterprise mobility maturity model.

- Level 1: This is an entry level for any enterprise to nourish mobility aspects. It is the level for an enterprise to prove itself as a mobile aware enterprise. The following are the key considerations for a level 1 enterprise:
  - [I.] key business policies
  - [II.] platform-specific policy
  - [III.] emails, contacts, calendar, and instant messaging (IM)
  - [IV.] basic mobile apps.

- Level 2: This is an intermediate level for an enterprise. It can also be called as mobile-enabled enterprise. The following are the key considerations for a level 2 enterprise:
  - [I.] end-to-end mobile solutions
  - [II.] enterprise policy
  - [III.] EMM (enterprise mobility management) tools and frameworks
  - [IV.] time-critical mobile apps
  - [V.] mobile device/app management
  - [VI.] cross-platform support
  - [VII.] well-defined business policies
  - [VIII.] mobile device data security.

- Level 3: This is an achiever or expert level for an enterprise with mobility aspects. Enterprises are known as mobile-engaged enterprises on this level. The following are the key considerations for a level 3 enterprise:
  - [I.] mobile trends–oriented, end-to-end mobile solution
  - [II.] enforced data security support
  - [III.] mobility-driven business innovations
  - [IV.] secure data gateway
  - [V.] enterprise app store
  - [VI.] measure results, feedbacks

[VII.]   communication and collaboration

[VIII.] integrated mobile device/app management

[IX.]   social networking

[X.]   well-defined and enforced device policy

[XI.]   strategy-driven road map

[XII.]   enforced business policies.

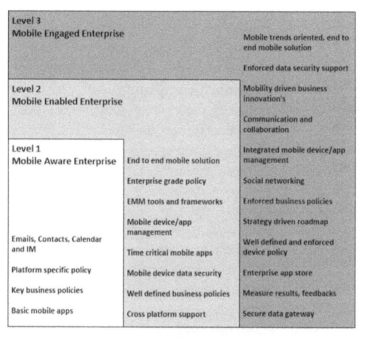

Figure 2-4: EM Maturity Model

The figure above illustrates the enterprise mobility maturity model. It depicts that consecutive levels also possess the properties of underlying level.

Maturity model is important for an enterprise to understand their level of mobility offerings. It also helps engaged stakeholders to define road maps and policies for enterprise mobility.

SUMMING UP

- ✓ An enterprise consists of
  - ➢ business departments
  - ➢ employees
  - ➢ stakeholders.
- ✓ Enterprise mobility ecosystem
  - ➢ Enterprise domain: finance, banking, health care, etc.
  - ➢ Enterprise core system: CRM, FSM, ESP, etc.
  - ➢ Mobile interface: iOS, Android, WP, etc.
- ✓ Enterprise mobility landscape
  - ➢ Needs: mobile extension of enterprise systems
  - ➢ Enablers: tools, technology, and frameworks
- ✓ Field service life cycle:
  - ➢ New appointment
  - ➢ Assign resource
  - ➢ Process/execute with resource tracking
  - ➢ Review/assess feedback
  - ➢ Close/complete flow
  - ➢ Analytics/reports
- ✓ CRM customer engagement steps: Lead → Opportunity → Account
- ✓ Enterprise mobility maturity model
  - ➢ Level 1: mobile aware enterprise
  - ➢ Level 2: mobile-enabled enterprise
  - ➢ Level 3: mobile-engaged enterprise

ACTION ITEMS

- ✓ Identify common features of CRM and ERP systems.
- ✓ Identify differences of ESS, SEP, and SCS systems.
- ✓ Why does an enterprise need ECM system?
- ✓ Identify differences of EIM and ECM systems.

3. ENTERPRISE MOBILITY MANAGEMENT

KEY POINTS COVERED

- ❖ Enterprise Mobility Management Overview
- ❖ EMM Suite and Its Components
- ❖ Enterprise Policies
- ❖ BYOD, CYOD, and COPE
- ❖ Enterprise App Store
- ❖ Mobile Email Management
- ❖ Mobile Content Management
- ❖ Mobile Expense Management
- ❖ Mobile Device Management
- ❖ Mobile Application Management
- ❖ EMM Console

One of the popular acronyms in the enterprise mobility ecosystem is EMM, which stands for enterprise mobility management. It primarily focuses on security and management of mobile apps, data, and devices. Mobile app deployment life cycle includes role-based access, installation, stores for application catalogue to end users, device distribution, configuration policies, etc. and comes under the horizon of EMM.

The concept and definition for enterprise mobility management emerged over time. It is still in an emerging state. EMM is a suite of solutions, services, strategies, and products. The figure below shows respective entities of EMM suites.

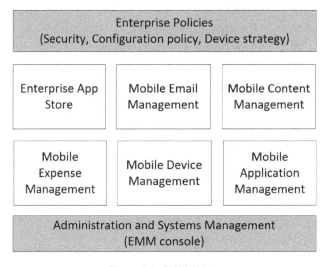

Figure 3-1: EMM Suites

Note

This section is important for understanding enterprise mobility. There are many EMM suite solutions/products available by market leaders.
••

3.1 Enterprise Policies

These are well-defined and documented enterprise policies for product, service, and solution usage by enterprise users. These policies are required to impose enterprise-grade security and configuration management.

3.1.1 Security and Configuration Policy

EMM basically focuses on security enforcement of enterprise data which are accessed by applications on a mobile device. There are security mechanisms which are required to be planned either with mobile applications or with other EMM components.

The following are some of the security mechanisms:

[I.]   built-in support for data encryption while in storage
[II.]   containerization implementation approach for applications
[III.] secure network communication.

The following are some of the configuration policies:

[I.]   VPN (virtual private network)
[II.]   firewall
[III.] SSO (single sign-on)
[IV.]   password protection
[V.]   certificate management
[VI.]   container management
[VII.] license management.

3.1.2 Device Strategy

It is essential to hold fine-grained and well-defined strategies for devices at enterprises. Emerging hardware and software capabilities of mobile devices have enlisted diverse device-distribution gateways. Enterprises can select and plan accordingly as per their motive and security-level enforcement. Each device-distribution approach requires a technical support system, application/device management, and admin console for administration activities and policies to enforce. Popular enterprise device strategies are BYOD, CYOD, and COPE, which are described below.

3.1.2.1 BYOD

Bring your own device (BYOD) is one of the popular device strategies with enterprises. In this approach, users are allowed to access their own personal devices for enterprise applications as enterprise data and applications are accessed via user's personal devices. So this strategy requires well-planned and enforced security to protect enterprise data.

3.1.2.2 CYOD

Choose your own device (CYOD) is the limited version of BYOD. In this device strategy, enterprises can support selected devices for application access and users are requested to choose a device out of proposed device list. This strategy would also demand security mechanisms and policies to protect enterprise data on devices.

3.1.2.3 COPE

Corporate-owned personally enabled (COPE) device-distribution policy is the way to ensure high level of security for enterprise data. This is also one of the recommended ways for enterprises if data is very sensitive and data loss may lead to high risk. Enterprises can harness customized COPE devices for a high-security mechanism and limited access for personal usage.

3.2 Enterprise App Store

Mobile applications expect a distribution platform for mobile application hosting. Each and every mobile platform supports a store for application deployment and installation on device (Google Play for Android apps, Apple store for iOS apps, Windows Phone Store for Windows Phone apps, etc.). These are consumer platforms which are developed and maintained for general usage of platform-specific devices. Some vendor-specific stores are also available, like Samsung store, Nokia Ovi store, and many more. Stores can be private with the specific objective of availability to restricted users. Any app store is not only limited to support mobile or desktop executables. It totally depends on store usage. However, under the EMM umbrella, enterprise app stores emphasize only on mobile applications.

Enterprises prefer to leverage private app stores due to security and user access management. Enterprise-specific application-distribution platforms are known as an enterprise app store. The following are some of the features for any EAS but not limited to:

[I.]   application version/life management
[II.]   submission, certification, etc.
[III.]   defined guidelines for deployment, approval
[IV.]   user profile and access management
[V.]   distribution management
[VI.]   cross-platform support
[VII.]   billing management
[VIII.]   alerts, notification, updates (OTA)
[IX.]   security
[X.]   analytics and reports
[XI.]   mobile device/application management
[XII.]   rating, review, and feedback.

EAS can be hosted on cloud or on premise as per system prerequisite. Store features and support may vary as per trends like BYOA (bring your own application), BYOD (bring your own device), etc. Enterprise app store is the platform to reach out enterprise users (partners, distributors, contractors, customers, or employees). It can even help to increase ROI (return on investment) of application portfolio. In the absence of an EAS, enterprise users have to deal with multiple consumer stores.

3.3 Mobile Email Management

Email access on mobile device is very basic facility for enterprise users. Email may incorporate sensitive enterprise data. Hence, it is the primary motive for any enterprise to own managed email access system. Mobile email management is the solution to provide secure and managed any time, anywhere email access to enterprise users at mobile devices.

The following are some of the features for mobile email management solution:

[I.]   email access strategy and policy
[II.]   integration with email platforms
[III.]   secure email access gateway
[IV.]   secure mechanism for attachment access
[V.]   data encryption support
[VI.]   remote access control and management.

Required features for mobile email management solution can also be integrated with other enablers (MDM, MAM, MCM, or other EMM components).

3.4 Mobile Content Management

Mobile content management (MCM) is the solution for secure and managed data access for a heterogeneous environment of smartphone, tablet, phablet, and other mobile devices. Enterprises may seek MCM catalyst for imposing enterprise-grade security mechanism for data and to prevent the system from data loss and theft.

The following are the imperative features for MCM system but not limited to:

[I.]   file storage
[II.]   data security mechanism at devices
[III.]   secure data gateway

[IV.]   data synchronization tools/platforms
[V.]   role-based data access management
[VI.]   real-time data availability
[VII.]   enterprise-grade data security mechanism and policies
[VIII.]   data protection mechanism and policies
[IX.]   remote data control (full wipe, selected wipe, backup, block, etc.)
[X.]   location-based data allocation.

MCM solution is a combination of versatile technologies, tools, and platforms which requires server- and client-side implementation. It can also be integrated with enterprise-level data management systems like ECM (enterprise content management) or CMS (content management system).

3.5 Mobile Expense Management

It is a solution for analyzing, tracking, and optimizing expenses of mobile usage at enterprise. Mobile expense management (MEM) is used for expense organization, control, and management for enterprise users. These expense management systems consider heterogeneous mobile devices (smartphones, tablets, and phablets). This solution is used by the account and finance department for budget management, and higher management consumes it for budget forecasting.

The following are the imperative features for any MEM solution but not limited to:

[I.]   analyzing, tracking, and alerting
[II.]   device inventory management
[III.]   mobile resource procurement
[IV.]   device usage tracking
[V.]   enterprise application usage analysis
[VI.]   network and data plan management
[VII.]   control misuse and abuse of enterprise services
[VIII.]   expense policy configuration and management

[IX.]   billing management

[X.]   budget audit and expense reports

[XI.]   budget forecast.

Proliferating usage of emails, SMS, texting, messengers, voice, and data require MEM systems for enterprise budget control and management.

3.6 Mobile Device Management

Enterprise application anticipates data security and real-time management of application/device. Mobile device management (MDM) is the approach for user-device management for data security and real-time device management.

The following are some of the imperative features offered by MDM but not limited to:

[I.]   device access management

[II.]   manage installed applications

[III.]   enable/disable device features/flows

[IV.]   identify and manage security controls

[V.]   real-time device monitoring/tracking with locations

[VI.]   remote lock/wipe device

[VII.]   policy management.

MDM solution or product possesses both server-side and mobile client-side handling. Server console sustains features to manage and control devices with respective configurations. These configurations or settings are communicated to client devices via respective protocols. And respective client implementation takes care for configuration management execution and other device-level security mechanism.

3.7 Mobile Application Management

Mobile application management (MAM) is the approach to serve enterprises imperative on the objective for data security and application management. As the name indicates, MAM emphasizes on application-level management, not at device level. MAM has emerged with BYOD/CYOD concepts because users would not prefer to carry enterprise MDM systems on his/her personal devices. However, an enterprise's application-specific security mechanism and policy enforcement can be accepted by users.

The following are some of the imperative features offered by MAM but not limited to:

[I.]   application access management
[II.]   manage application life cycle
[III.] enable/disable application features/business flow
[IV.]   application data security while data is at rest
[V.]   real-time application monitoring
[VI.]   data wipe on the go
[VII.] remote resume/suspend application.

This solution approach requires a server-side system and respective client-side handling to achieve the desired features. Server-side system along with admin console and client at device communicates via ubiquitous protocols. These protocols provide control at servers for managing enterprise application.

3.8 Administration and Systems Management

EMM suite moderates different components/systems for managing enterprise mobile applications. Management and administration over these systems would also be required. EMM console is intended for such purpose. It is feasible to hold common console for administration and management of diverse EMM systems (MAM, MDM, and EAS). It is preferred and very common for EMM solutions to leverage one generic EMM console consisting of MAM, MDM, and EAS for their administration and management which facilitate the enterprise for mobile application life cycle management.

SUMMING UP

✓ EMM is a suite consisting of EAS, MAM, MDM, MEM, MCM, secure email, policies, and administrator console.

✓ EMM solution approach depends on the enterprise's device environment (BYOD, CYOD, COPE, or other).

✓ The enterprise app store is the platform for enterprise application submission, access, installation, and management.

✓ Mobile email management is the solution for an enterprise's imperative attempt of secure email any time, anywhere access and management.

✓ Mobile content management is used for centralized enterprise data management, security enforcement, and prevention of data loss and theft.

✓ Analyzing, tracking, alerting, monitoring, and reporting mobile expenses are done by mobile expense management solution.

✓ Mobile device management is the solution for imposing device-level security control and management. It is preferred if enterprise data is very sensitive.

✓ Mobile application management solution facilitates application-level security control and management. It can be easily used with BYOD, CYOD, and any other approaches.

✓ EMM console is the common platform for EMM suite systems administration and management.

ACTION ITEMS

- ✓ What are the differences among enterprise mobility and enterprise mobility management?
- ✓ Is it feasible to use MDM solution with BYOD?
- ✓ What are the parameters to choose among assorted device strategies (BYOD, CYOD, and COPE) for enterprise environment?
- ✓ Prepare comparative case study of existing app stores and their features.

4. TECHNOLOGY STAKE

KEY POINTS COVERED

- ❖ Deployment Approaches
- ❖ Mobile Platforms (Android, iOS, Windows Phone, BlackBerry)
- ❖ Mobile Platform Customization
- ❖ Mobile Devices and Form Factors (Feature Phone, SmartPhone, Tablets, Phablets)
- ❖ Mobile Application Classification and Definition
- ❖ Mobile Hybrid Application Concept and Overview
- ❖ IVR Application Overview

Technologies for enterprise mobility is not limited or bounded any more. There can be traditional old approaches or legacy systems working for an enterprise, or it may be an emerging ecosystem. In a mobility horizon, there can be two broad divisions, which can be defined as server components and client components. Here, server includes all the databases handling, desktop executables, admin consoles, web infrastructure, etc. For all such components, deployment mechanism is also an important perspective for enterprise system accomplishment. The following are the three approaches for making server components deployed and customizing them for client apps:

[I.]   On premise: In this scenario, deployment is done under enterprise secured network, database store, and access. Everything comes under the enterprise network and premises. Here, the enterprise manages all the deployed components. It can be outsourced also but with well-defined policies and security mechanism. This approach requires infrastructure setup and management at enterprise premise. These on-premise systems can be customized as per enterprise system state.

[II.]   Cloud: One of the popular and proliferating approaches with emerging demand is cloud computing. Cloud hosting means accessing data and services via online rather than accessing data and services from in-house network. This basically facilitates enterprise data and applications hosted on cloud. These cloud systems are customizable and scalable as per enterprise objectives. Cloud computing avails software components as a service to clients or users. These clouds can be a private cloud to the enterprise or even separate hosting on a public cloud. Combination of private and public cloud can also be feasible options for enterprises. SAAS (Software as a Service) is a wide consideration for enterprise. There are multiple technical aspects with cloud computing besides distributed database, multitenancy, etc.

[III.]   Hybrid: It's not always feasible for enterprises to go with on-premise or cloud hosting for all systems required for their execution. So a combination of both as per enterprise system state is known as a hybrid. This gives advantages of both the hosting approaches and reduces dependency on one solution approach. Hybrid approach introduces versatile flexibilities to enterprises, besides secure data and services hosting, at on-premise while adequate information can be shared via cloud hosting.

All these hosting and deployment procedures are considered as server components. Later in this section, we would emphasize more on client components and their technologies.

4.1 Mobile Platforms

Mobile platforms are emerging and evolving with versatile technology innovations. There is no common or universally accepted single platform for mobile devices. It varies from country to country. However, there are few mobile device platforms which capture the majority of the market among the world.

4.1.1 Android

Android is a mobile operating system by Google, designed primarily for devices as touchscreen mobiles and tablets, with specialized versions for TV (Android TV), cars (Android Auto), and wearable devices (Android Wear). It is one of the leading mobile operating systems. Android source code has been released under open-source license. Google Play distributes applications to Android device users. The following are the features supported on Android OS (operating system):

[I.]   barcode reader

[II.]   OCR (optical character recognition) integration

[III.]   NFC (near field communication) wallets

[IV.]   LBS (location-based services) based navigation, directions

[V.]   map view, geotracking/tagging/fencing

[I.]   push notification—GCM (Google Cloud Messaging), C2DM (cloud-to-device messaging)

[VI.]   data sharing across applications using content provider

[VII.]   relational database support—SQLite.

The following are the guidelines which should be taken care of while designing and implementation of Android application:

[I.]   Common installer for diverse Android OS, form factors, and devices with:
   o backward compatibility feature support for different Android OS
   o flexible and adaptive UI (user interface) design for heterogeneous devices (single/multipane devices, diverse screen resolutions/sizes).

By using Android-supported features, distinctive applications can be implemented like:

[II.]   interactive UI-based charting, reporting applications

[III.]   relational database intensive application, high-performance SQLite-based applications

[IV.]   native widget development

[V.]   UI customization for rich UI- and animation-based applications with features like view, drag and drop, list reordering, etc.

[VI.]   native development using NDK (native development kit).

4.1.2 iOS

iOS is a mobile operating system by Apple, distributed with Apple hardware devices, previously known as iPhone OS, and later on distributed with iPad, iPod, and Apple TV. iOS mobile applications are distributed to users by Apple store. The following are the features supported on iOS:

[I.]   barcode reader
[II.]   OCR (optical character recognition) integration
[III.]   NFC (near field communication) wallets
[IV.]   LBS (location-based services) based navigation, directions
[V.]   map view, geotracking/tagging/fencing
[VI.]   push notification—APNS (Apple Push Notification service)
[VII.]   relational database support—SQLite.

By using iOS supported features, distinctive applications can be implemented like:

[I.]   relational database intensive application using NSCoreData
[II.]   interactive info graphical data representation application
[III.]   native application development using Cocoa Touch (Apple's native object-oriented application programming interface)
[IV.]   custom, configurable implementation for leveraging device hardware capabilities
[V.]   application profiling/test automation using instrument
[VI.]   universal application development for iPad and iPhone.

4.1.3 Windows Phone

Windows Phone is a smartphone operating system by Microsoft. It is successor to Windows Mobile OS, which was primarily focused for enterprise market users. However, Windows Phone OS primarily focuses on consumer market users. It is based on Metro design guidelines. Windows Phone applications are distributed via Windows Phone Store. The following are the features supported on WP:

[I.]   barcode reader

[II.]   OCR (optical character recognition) integration

[III.] NFC (near field communication) wallets

[IV.]   LBS (location-based services) based navigation, directions

[V.]   map view, geotracking/tagging/fencing

[VI.]   push notification—WNS (Windows Push Notification Service).

By using Windows OS supported features, distinctive applications can be implemented like:

[I.]   custom, configurable implementation for leveraging device hardware capabilities

[II.]   UI customization for rich UI- and animation-based applications

[III.] co-development of Windows Presentation Foundation (WPF) applications for multiple platforms via

   o   segregating platform independent business code in respective MVVM (Model-View-ViewModel) approach

   o   separating entire business code in common portable class library (PCL) compatible with all the platforms (WPF platforms)

[IV.]   Expression Studio usage for

   o   UX designing and rapid prototyping

   o   data binding with MVVM

[V.]   application development for Windows with managed and unmanaged code.

4.1.4 BlackBerry

BlackBerry was one of the leading platforms for enterprise users before Android and iOS captured the market. The QWERTY keypad mobile devices with BlackBerry OS by RIM (Research in Motion) were considered the most enterprise-grade devices, with BES (BlackBerry Enterprise Server) security management. The following are the features supported on BB (BlackBerry) platform:

[I.]   barcode reader
[II.]   OCR (optical character recognition) integration
[III.]   NFC (near field communication) wallets
[IV.]   LBS (location-based services) based navigation, directions
[V.]   map view, geotracking/tagging/fencing
[VI.]   BB push notifications
[VII.]   cloud storage
[VIII.] cache management using persistent store, RMS (Records Management System), file system, etc.
[IX.]   BlackBerry Enterprise Server (BES) support and monitoring
[X.]   BlackBerry Internet Service (BIS).

By using BlackBerry platform supported features, distinctive applications can be implemented like:

[I.]   custom, configurable implementation for leveraging device hardware capabilities
[II.]   advanced and seamless user interface
[III.]   advanced graphics/navigation UI's (tabbed) similar to iPhone, with the help of prefabricated components
[IV.]   BBM (BlackBerry Messenger) connected apps
[V.]   application development using Java, QNX, Adobe Air, and Webworks

[VI.] protocol stack implementation, like RTSP (Real-Time Streaming Protocol) and RTP (Real-Time Transport Protocol).

There are many other platforms available in the market (Firefox OS, Samsung Bada, Symbian, etc.).

4.2 Mobile Platform Customization

Enterprises can gestate mobile platform customization for fine-grained or tailored control on mobile devices. Corporate-owned devices can be enterprise-ready customized mobile platform devices. These devices can be administrated and managed by admin console to enforce enterprise policies on devices. Enterprise-ready customized platform embeds control of the devices, applications, and role-based access, which enforce high level of security management. Mobile platform customization can leverage the following aspects:

[I.] custom branding and UI/UX
[II.] add or remove device features from platform
[III.] integration with third-party hardware devices
[IV.] install, remove, or upgrade applications on platform
[V.] platform porting and upgrade
[VI.] integrate legacy code
[VII.] Firmware Over-the-Air (FOTA) installation or upgrade.

Such mobile platform customization catalysts can also be leveraged by OEMs (original equipment manufacturer), either for the enterprise or consumer market.

4.3 Mobile Devices and Form Factors

Evolving hardware capabilities are the major cause for rapidly changing mobile devices and their availability with diverse form factors.

[I.]   Feature phone: These are basic phones with limited feature set. Mainly used for voice calls and SMS with system apps (calendar, alarm, games, etc.).

[II.]   Smartphone: They are mobile computing devices generally with screen size less than 5.3 inches. They have obsoleted the use of PDA devices. It has applications and features to manage personal and professional works. The latest hardware capabilities of smartphones also incorporate high computing processors, storages, and memory units.

[III.] Tablets: Touchscreen devices with screen size from 7.0 to 10 inches. They are the minicomputers with capabilities like Internet connection, applications, data storage, video/audio players, etc.

[IV.]   Phablets: These devices generally contain screen size from 5.3 to 6.9 inches. The word *phablet* has been coined for devices which come between smartphone and tablet.

4.4 Mobile Applications

Mobile applications broadly can be divided into two forms as system apps and third-party apps. System apps are those applications which come inbuilt with mobile operating systems or platforms. However, third-party apps are those applications which are implemented and installed by the developer community.

4.4.1 System Apps

Applications implemented with NDK (native development kit), which can be integrated with mobile platforms or OS, are system apps. Each platform provides NDK or other approaches for implementing system apps. Applications provided by default from platforms on devices are system apps, which are either implemented by the platform community or partner vendor. For example, Android provides NDK which supports system apps implementation via C/C++ programming language, while Android SDK (software development kit) supports native application implementation via Java programming language.

System apps are efficient enough to program application at hardware-level interactions and optimizations like memory, process, execution, etc.

4.4.2 Third-Party Apps

There are several development approaches for implementing third-party mobile applications. It can be classified in three types as:

[I.]   native apps
[II.]   web apps
[III.]   hybrid apps.

4.4.2.1 Native Apps

They are also known as thick client applications. These applications are implemented via mobile device platform native technologies (Android, iOS, Windows Phone, or other). Here are the imperative characteristics for mobile native app:

[I.]   an executable file installs and resides at the mobile device
[II.]   executed directly by mobile operating system
[III.]   able to use mobile platform or operating system APIs
[IV.]   distributed via platform-specific app store or via enterprise distribution mechanism.

4.4.2.2 Web Apps

They are also known as thin client applications. These apps are implemented with web technologies (HTML, CSS, and JavaScript). Some imperative characteristics for mobile web app are:

[I.]   apps are executed by the device browser of mobile operating system

[II.]   app can leverage only limited device features for application implementation

[III.]   app doesn't carry any executable file which can be installed or removed from mobile OS

4.4.2.3 Hybrid Apps

Hybrid applications are neither native apps nor web apps. They are implemented with web technologies and packaged as applications for distribution. These apps can access native device features and APIs. Basically a hybrid app is a native mobile application which hosts a web browser control within its main UI screen. Here are the imperative characteristics for mobile hybrid app:

[I.]   UI implementation using web technologies (HTML, CSS, and JavaScript)

[II.]   apps are capable to use mobile platform or operating system APIs

[III.]   an executable file installs and resides at the mobile device

[IV.]   apps can be distributed via platform-specific app store or enterprise distribution mechanism.

The figure below depicts an analogy of hybrid application. Broadly it has two layers, as container and user interface, where container is implemented on native mobile technology (Android, iOS, or Windows Phone). UI (user interface) is implemented with web technologies (HTML, CSS, and JS).

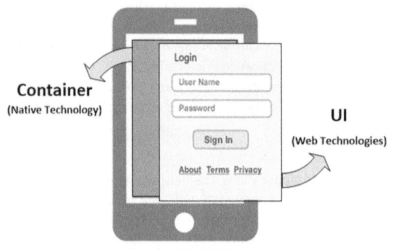

Figure 4-1: Mobile Hybrid App

There are many frameworks and tools for hybrid app application development. The major selling point for the hybrid app is its cross-platform development. The following are the features which can be leveraged with a hybrid app:

[I.]   integration of open-source frameworks with HTML5
[II.]   liquid layouts for multiscreen UIs
[III.] local storage, multimedia handling, semantics and forms, graphics, etc.
[IV.]   a single code-based architecture model for multiplatform presentations
[V.]   hybrid framework that bundles the HTML5 based view layer, with native platform containers to create deployable builds.

4.4.3 Other Apps

There are other distinctive ways of information communication to mobile devices, like SMS (Short Message Service) and IVR (interactive voice response).

4.4.3.1 SMS-Based

This is short-code based SMS application. In this application, the user is required to send SMS in specified short-code to avail services. These kinds of applications are primarily driven by network operator and SMS server to extend the application services for feature phones.

4.4.3.2 IVR Apps

IVR applications are used for automated interactions with callers. They are basically used for customer support department to avail services 24/7. These applications are multilingual to serve customers across heterogeneous regions. IVR apps are driven by network operator and IVR servers; it doesn't require any additional client application to install on mobile phones.

Enterprises are looking towards IVR application to reduce TCO (total cost of ownership) with sales, collections, inquiries, and other services.

The figure below illustrates generic layer structure for a typical IVR application.

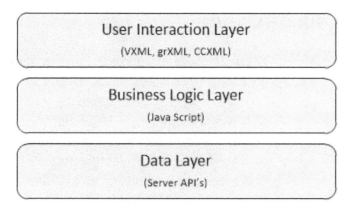

Figure 4-2: IVR App

In general an IVR application consists of three layers as:

[I.]   User Interaction Layer: This layer uses VXML (voice extensible markup language), CCXML (call control extensible markup language), and GRXML (grammar extensible markup language) for interactive voice conversation. VXML is used for direct interaction with a caller. CCXML is used for call control like call setup, monitoring, tear down phone calls, etc. Grammar validations are done with GRXML where user can provide his/her inputs via speech or DTMF (dual-tone multifrequency) codes. These VXML, CCXML, and grammars are designed and implemented as per application desired feat.

[II.]   Business Logic Layer: This layer is used for all sorts of application-specific network communication and data needs. This is implemented inside VXML using <script> tag with JavaScript programming.

[III.] Data Layer: This layer represents diverse data sources interaction layer used by IVR application. IVR application uses respective server APIs to fetch relevant data from required data sources or CMS (content management system).

SUMMING UP

✓   There are several approaches for enterprise server hosting (on-premise, cloud, or hybrid).

✓   Popular mobile platforms across the world are Android, iOS, Windows Phone, and BlackBerry.

✓   Mobile platform customization is the way to achieve high level of security for enterprises.

✓   There are diverse kinds of mobile devices and form factors (feature phone, smartphone, tablet, and phablet).

✓   Mobile applications broadly can be classified in two forms as system applications and third-party applications.

- ✓ Native applications are thick client applications which are implemented via mobile device platform native technologies (Android, iOS, or Windows Phone).
- ✓ Web applications are thin client applications with limited access to mobile platform capabilities. They are implemented by using web technologies (HTML, CSS, and JavaScript).
- ✓ Hybrid applications are amalgamation of native and web technologies. They are implemented with web technologies and packaged as native application.
- ✓ IVR applications are driven by the network operator for automated interactions with callers.

ACTION ITEMS

- ✓ Identify popular mobile platforms or OS specific to countries (India, USA, UK, Japan, and China).
- ✓ List down the differences among tablet and phablet.
- ✓ Why would an enterprise opt for mobile platform customization?
- ✓ List down the differences among mobile thin client and thick client.
- ✓ Identify popular UI frameworks for mobile hybrid app development.
- ✓ Identify the real-time scenario for SMS-based applications at an enterprise ecosystem.
- ✓ List down the features supported by the latest Windows Phone operating system.
- ✓ List down the features supported by the latest Android operating system.
- ✓ List down the features supported by the latest iOS operating system.
- ✓ What is Android ONE?
- ✓ What are the swift programming language features?

5. ENTERPRISE MOBILE APP ARCHITECTURE

KEY POINTS COVERED

- ❖ Mobile Application Architecture
- ❖ Information Flow
- ❖ Application Layer Structure
- ❖ Architecture Components
- ❖ Unified Push Notification
- ❖ mBaaS Overview
- ❖ MEAP Overview
- ❖ SOA Overview
- ❖ Authentication Mechanism for Enterprise Applications

Enterprise mobile application blueprint is gestated for hassle-free footprints while execution with real systems. It is challenging to identify an application's first-version features, with considerations for scalability, expandability, and flexibility. Minimum viable product (MVP) is the term coined for such scenarios where enterprises can plan the first version of an application with minimum required features for target users. Features of the application can be limited. However, architecture and design should be scalable, expandable, and flexible. Mobile application design and architecture requires precise consideration for factors like:

[I.]   type of application
[II.]   target user segments
[III.]   target mobile platforms and device form factors
[IV.]   features of application
[V.]   localization
[VI.]   communication channels (push notification, SMS, IVR)
[VII.]   hybrid versus native versus web client app
[VIII.] middleware support and services (cloud-hosted or on-premise)
[IX.]   security mechanism
[X.]   enterprise device environment (BYOD, COPE, CYOD)
[XI.]   device platform customization
[XII.]   application distribution channel (EAS or consumer platform specific stores)
[XIII.] MAM or MDM support
[XIV.]   mobile trends (mobile first, gamification, etc.).

There can be many other major or minor entities which can influence overall application architecture and design.

Note

This section considers mobile application architecture and design with basic entities and feature sets. However, it may seek some amendments as per real environment application-specific needs.

●●

5.1 Information Flow

Internet is one of the basic components for any mobile application, as most of the mobile applications are client–server applications. There can be very specific motives to design client-only mobile applications without any server communication channel. For client–server applications, there are multiple channels of communication of information to mobile-client application like SMS (Short Message Service), push notification, IVR (interactive voice response), and server APIs. The figure below exemplifies SMS/IVR gateway and basic client–server application communication flow. However, push notification is detailed out later in this section.

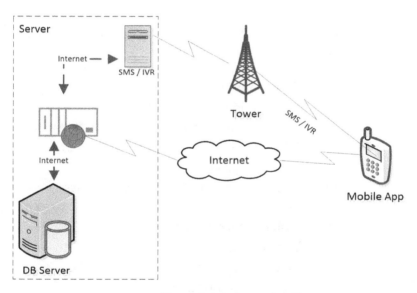

Figure 5-1: Information Flow

5.2 Enterprise Mobile App Components

Enterprise mobile app design and architecture requires consideration of assorted components and participating entities.

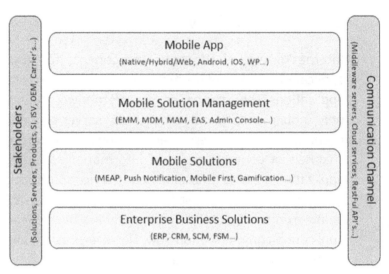

Figure 5-2: Enterprise Mobile App Components

The following are the components for enterprise mobile application:

[I.]   Stakeholders: Individual persons, groups, or organizations which affect or get affected by targeting enterprise mobile applications are the stakeholders. They are systems integrator, ISV, OEMs, and other solutions, products, or services.

[II.]   Enterprise Business Solutions: These are the core infrastructure components, over which enterprise mobile application can be designed. These business software solutions are the real executor of business execution in enterprise like ERP, CRM, SCM, FSM.

[III.] Mobile Solutions: There are respective standard approaches and tools available for mobile application design and development. They also consider leading mobile trends (mobile first, gamification, and others). All these solutions, tools, and frameworks are required to be considered while designing a mobile application or solution. And they can be used as per enterprise mobile applications desired features.

[IV.]   Mobile Solution Management: Designed solution anticipates adequate level of security, management, and administrative actions while execution. Assorted tools and frameworks should be considered while enterprise mobile app design phase like EMM, MDM/MAM, EAS, admin console.

[V.]   Mobile App: This is the final outcome as a mobile application which is used by target users. It requires consideration of diverse available mobile platform, popular devices, and form factors. Selection among application type (native, hybrid, or web) is also required, as per target segments and application features.

[VI.]   Communication Channel: This is the layer for communicating information among respective components. These are basically middleware servers, cloud services, RESTful APIs, and communication protocols to establish connection between different components and layers of end-to-end enterprise mobile app solution.

5.3 Enterprise Mobile App Architecture

A generic approach for enterprise mobile application architecture is presented here. However, it can be articulated as per real-time application features and participating entities.

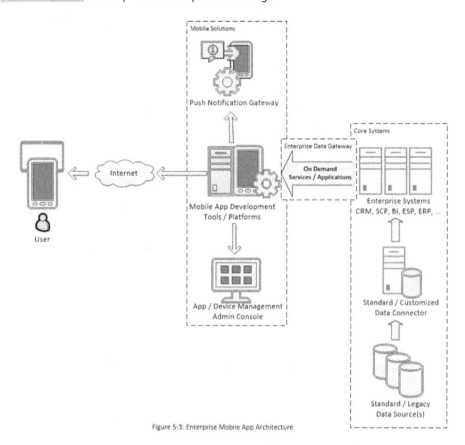

Figure 5-3: Enterprise Mobile App Architecture

In general, enterprise mobile application architecture can be classified in multiple segments as:

[I.]   Core Systems: This is the core system of an enterprise with respective working systems (ERP, CRM, SCP, FSM, etc.). An enterprise may consist of standard legacy databases with database connectors for business roots incorporation. Integration with heterogeneous systems in the form of services/databases reckons on enterprise existing solutions.

[II.]   Mobile Solutions: This is the combination and collaboration of versatile mobile tools, technologies, and frameworks, which are required to implement mobile applications. They communicate with enterprise systems via exposed services and applications.

[III.]   Enterprise Data Gateway: An enterprise core system exposes services and applications under the secure data gateway communication.

[IV.]   End Users: Mobile applications across heterogeneous platforms and form factors are accessed by end users via platform stores or enterprise app stores.

Enterprise mobile application architecture is not emphasizing on MEAP, EMM, or mBaaS because they are not the compulsory component to build enterprise mobile apps though the above architecture illustrates the basis components and participating entities. MEAP, EMM, and mBaaS are discussed separately in respective sections.

5.4 App Layer Structure

Mobile application incorporates multiple layers to entertain in one application codebase.

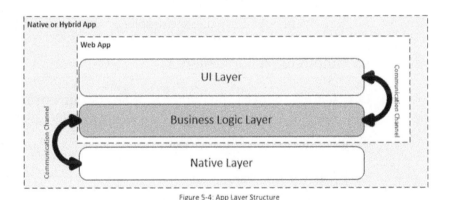

Figure 5-4: App Layer Structure

The figure illustrates three distinctive layers as:

[I.]   UI Layer: This layer represents UI/UX and view implementation for mobile application. Native platforms support their respective ways of implementation approach for UI layer. Hybrid and web application UI layer is implemented with HTML, CSS,

JS, and other UI frameworks/tools (jQuery, jQuery Mobile, LESS, Bootstrap, etc.). This is the layer where platform-specific UI/UX guidelines are required to implement as per application features.

[II.]   Business Logic Layer: This layer is responsible for core logic and implementation handling for application. It also communicates with the server for required data and information. Respective design patterns and architectures can be used as per platform recommendations and application features, like Singleton, MVC (Model View Controller), MVVM (Model-View-ViewModel). In case of cross-platform development, it is recommended to harness common business logic layer among platform-specific builds.

[III.]   Native Layer: This layer takes care of platform-specific capabilities (camera, database, HTTP communication, persistent store, etc.) to be used by mobile application. This layer is not accessible with web application implementation. This is the reason web applications possess limited access to mobile platform capabilities.

5.5 Architecture Ingredients

This section details out other important infrastructure ingredients or components which are required while working on end-to-end solutions for mobile applications.

5.5.1 Push Notification

Client–server communication is an imperative need in today's era of Internet where user demands access of data and information from anywhere at any time. Client-server communication can be done with either pull or push mechanism. In pull technology, client application requests server for specific data in proper format. And it receives a formatted response from server. In push technology, data communication occurs to client from server. Basic difference within pull and push is the communication mechanism. Pull communication is initiated by client, while push communication is initiated by server. Though, timer-based pull mechanism implementation at background gives the assumption of push communication, and it is used by some applications or solutions.

Push notification is the server-initiated communication to client applications in which the server has details (client identifier and application identifier) to communicate. It is very common to observe push notification on the mobile notification bar, where it notifies for new mails and updates. Push notification works even if application is not on running state at client side.

Push notification is one of the important perspectives and parts of solution for enterprise systems where the server sends data/information at the right time to its user. Push notification implementation at mobile-client application requires understanding of heterogeneous platform specific communication protocols. Push notification basically relies on the server to possess a unique identifier for each mobile user which can be used to communicate information. These push notification communication is supported by distinctive protocols with heterogeneous platforms, like APNS (Apple Push Notification service) at iOS; GCM (Google Cloud Messaging), and C2DM (Cloud-to-device messaging) at Android; and WNS (Windows Push Notification Service) at WP devices.

Below is the diagram for unified push notification support. UPN communicates with the application server as per enterprise system state.

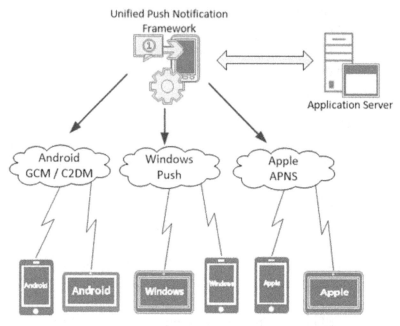

Figure 5-5: Unified Push Notification

Cross-platform support at mobile client application anticipates UPN (unified push notification) gateway and framework for implementation support where UPN framework is intended for a common layer above platform-specific protocols. This is expected to deal with common message communication among heterogeneous platform devices. The following are some of the benefits with UPN:

[I.]   lesser maintenance efforts at server end
[II.]   easier to push message across multiple platforms
[III.]   consistency in delivered message
[IV.]   reduced latency in message delivery
[V.]   better tracking of registered devices and their current activeness.

5.5.2 Single Sign-on

Enterprises have multiple systems to be accessed by users. These systems are intended for distinctive purposes and objectives. Only authenticated users are allowed to access systems. Authentication plays an important role in the enterprise ecosystem. It helps to enforce security mechanism as per user role and access rights.

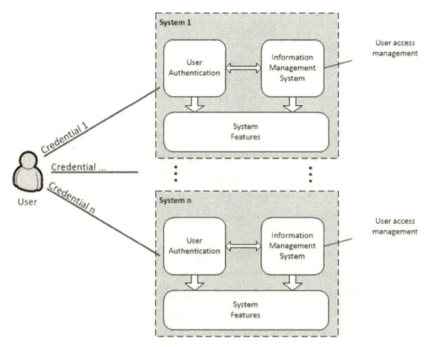

Figure 5-6: Legacy Authentication Approach

The diagram above depicts the legacy approach for authentication used by enterprises for heterogeneous systems. Such legacy systems possess separate user credentials for distinctive systems authentication. Sign-on is required on respective systems for feature access by user. These systems sustain their own authentication and user access management handling.

Single sign-on (SSO) is the approach to handle authentication mechanism for multiple systems accessed by users. It provides single credentials and authentication layer to users. Only a one-time sign-on is required to access distinctive systems by user.

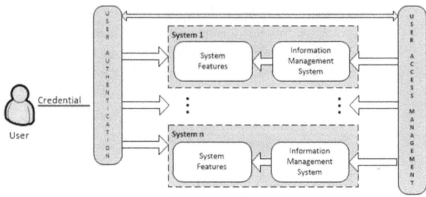

Figure 5-7: Single Sign-on

The diagram above illustrates the components in case of single sign-on approach. In this scenario, there can be a common user access management system, which empowers single sign-on authentication to end users. It can also communicate respective information to enterprise systems.

Single sign-on is the independent module which can be integrated with distinctive systems within an enterprise for user authentication. There are multiple ways for implementation approach to leverage single sign-on. Integration with LDAP (lightweight directory access protocol) is one of the ways.

5.5.2.1 LDAP

Lightweight directory access protocol (LDAP) is the industry standard for directory services for enterprises. By using LDAP system, enterprise user's profile, setting, contact details, etc. can be organized and shared among distinctive enterprise systems. It provides secure and centrally organized enterprise users information, which helps to achieve real-time updates to integrated enterprise systems. Integration with single sign-on is one of the common usages for the LDAP system.

5.5.3 mBaaS

Mobile Backend as a Service (mBaaS) is basically cloud-based offering for backend handling. It is an alternative for mobile middleware, also popularly known as Backend as a Service (BaaS). Mobile applications communication with on-premise physical servers was the traditional approach. mBaaS offers server on cloud for connecting client applications at connected devices (mobile, tablet, and web). Enterprises can opt for private, public, or hybrid cloud depending on business objectives.

mBaaS can be classified in two forms as:

[I.]   consumer mBaaS
[II.]   enterprise mBaaS.

Consumer and enterprise mBaaS offers different features and services due to diverse business objectives. Respective palming and planning would be expected by each of consumer and enterprise mBaaS systems.

There are two introductory features for any mBaaS system as:

[I.]   storage for data
[II.]   RESTful APIs with CRUD (create, read, update, and delete) operations on (consumer/enterprise) data.

In addition to the imperative features, mBaaS may carry other versatile features as:

[I.]   user management
[II.]   authentication and access control
[III.]   usage analytics
[IV.]   push notification
[V.]   geolocation
[VI.]   social network
[VII.]   security and versioning

[VIII.] integration with enterprise standard database systems.

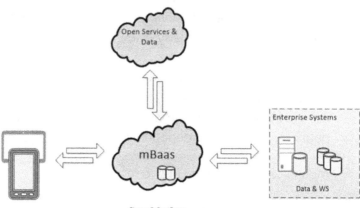

Figure 5-8: mBaas

The figure exemplifies the flow with mBaaS as a replacement for middle-layer servers where it communicates to enterprise systems for required services and information. It can also fetch details from other cloud sources, like social platforms for any open data and services. Mobile clients can expect respective web services from mBaaS for relevant CRUD operations and information. mBaaS also persists data as per system design.

In the era of user empowerments and transformational mobility solutions, mBaaS is a belligerent for enterprises. It can be one of the core building blocks for enterprises to harness unified communication among connected devices. It provides assorted benefits as:

[I.]   unified communication with connected devices
[II.]   cross mobile platform support
[III.] rapid time-to-market
[IV.]   easy backend management
[V.]   easy integration.

5.5.4 MEAP

Mobile enterprise application platform (MEAP) is an acronym for a products and services suite used for mobile applications development. It is basically a set of middleware tools and frameworks for managing end-to-end mobile app life cycle. It recommends a common codebase for multiple-platform mobile apps. One of the major benefits of MEAP suite is cross-platform support which is one of the leading challenges of enterprise mobility. MEAP systems can be cloud-hosted and availed as a service for enterprise use. The following are the features of any MEAP suite:

[I.]   cross-platform support

[II.]   support and manage diversified devices and form factors

[III.]   long-term approach for mobile application development and deployment

[IV.]   rapid mobile application development infrastructure

[V.]   built-in support for integration with backend database systems

[VI.]   configurable development toolsets

[VII.]   centrally managed mobile applications

[VIII.]   management of mobile app life cycle from development, testing, and deployment.

Rule of three is considered as a must for any MEAP system. The following are the 'rule of three' statements:

[I.]   System should support at least three mobile applications

[II.]   System should support at least three mobile operating systems

[III.]   System should support at least integration with three backend database systems.

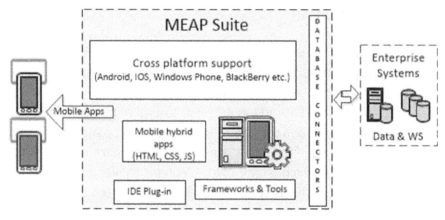

Figure 5-9: MEAP

MEAP suite is an integration of versatile tools, frameworks, IDE (integrated development environment) plug-ins, and standard database connectors for enterprise systems which are used for cross-platform support and mobile hybrid apps implementation.

5.5.5 SOA

Service-oriented architecture (SOA) is a design pattern for application development. It is not specific to mobile or any technology. It is an implementation approach which emphasizes on service implementation in application architecture where a service is an independent, loosely coupled, and self-contained functionality of a system. It can be integrated with many technologies, frameworks, and protocols as per system design.

Below is the figure for service-oriented architecture. It is a design pattern and can be used with big data, social, cloud, mobile, or other applications. As the figure illustrates, a system can harness many self-contained services which can be repetitively executed by business systems. These services interact with enterprise data sources, components, and other modules as per system design.

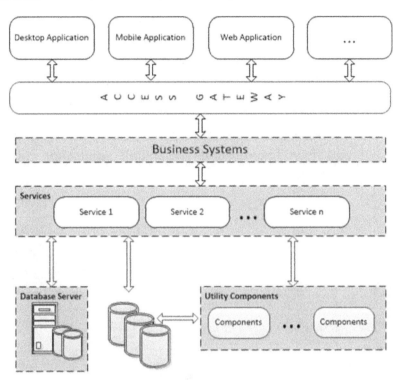

Figure 5-10: Service Oriented Architecture

Note

This is a generic diagram for SOA overview, and it may need amendments for dissimilar systems.

SOA is widely used with mobile- and cloud-based applications for rapid development and enhancement. It facilitates scalability, manageability, and robustness in the application architecture. For an enterprise, it is important to harness pluggable and independent modules/components. SOA is the architecture approach to provide agility for transformation of system as and when needed.

5.5.6 EMM Powered Application

EMM is elaborated on section 3 with overview, component, and feature. Here, the intent is to cover architecture for enterprise application powered by EMM solution.

The figure below exemplifies participating entities, components, and flows for implementing mobile application with EMM solutions.

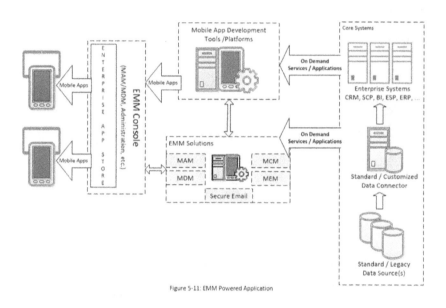

Figure 5-11: EMM Powered Application

The following are the participating entities for EMM powered application development:

[I.]   Core Systems: This is the enterprise core system infrastructure setup. It exposes required services, applications as desired by enterprise mobile application.

[II.]   EMM Solutions: These are solutions for application or device management. They are planned and implemented for imposing required security, control, and management for enterprise-grade application.

Enterprises may opt for existing popular EMM solution as per system state and objective.

[III.] Mobile App Development Tools/Platforms: These are sets of tools, platforms, and frameworks for mobile application development. For EMM powered application, these development approaches require close coordination with EMM solutions, which are identified for enterprise application.

[IV.] EMM Console: Enterprise users can download mobile client applications from EAS. Mobile application and device management is done by EMM console. This console is managed by authorized enterprise users for policies and configurations with enterprise applications.

Selection among EMM suite components (MAM, MDM, MCM, MEM, EAS, etc.) for enterprise application development depends on enterprise system state and objective. Even enterprises may opt for only selected features out of EMM solution—for example, enterprise application development with EAS and MAM features.

SUMMING UP

✓ There are various information flow channels (SMS, IVR, push notification, and server APIs) for mobile applications.

✓ Enterprise mobile application requires consideration of respective components like:
  ➢ stakeholders (solutions, services, products, etc.)
  ➢ communication channel (cloud, on-premise, etc.)
  ➢ mobile app (native/hybrid/web)
  ➢ mobile solution management (EMM, M(X)M, EAS, etc.)
  ➢ mobile solutions (MEAP, mobile first, etc.)
  ➢ enterprise business solutions (ERP, CRM, SCM, etc.)

✓ Enterprise data gateway is the secure way of transforming data and services via Internet for communication with client applications and other architecture components.

✓ Push notifications are server-initiated communication to client applications where the server gets details (client application and device identifiers) while registration.

✓ Unified push notification is the approach to leverage common gateway or communication channel for cross-platform support.

✓ SSO is the secure implementation approach and protocol as authentication system for accessing multiple systems by users.

✓ LDAP is the standard way for enterprises to possess a common mechanism of accessing users' (employees, partners, customers, etc.) profile and respective data.

✓ mBaaS is a cloud-based service offering as an alternate for mobile middleware servers.

✓ MEAP is a suite of products, services, tools, and frameworks for mobile application development.

✓ SOA is a design pattern used for rapid development and enhancement in mobile application.

ACTION ITEMS

✓ Identify scenarios to hold IVR applications at enterprises' mobile solutions.

✓ What are the limitations or security threat to use SSO?

✓ When and why should mBaaS be used for enterprise mobile solutions?

✓ Identify any open-source third-party tool or framework for unified push notification.

✓ Is LDAP compulsory for any enterprise solutions to possess common mechanism for accessing user details?

6. TRENDS

KEY POINTS COVERED

- ❖ Mobile First
- ❖ Gamification Overview
- ❖ Wearable Devices at Enterprises
- ❖ Hybrid
- ❖ IOT Overview and Classification

In this era of globalization, there are many factors other than technology, hardware, or software, which directly or indirectly influences the system approaches. They are known as trends. Enterprise mobility is not an exception; it acts upon such trends. This section details out the trends among enterprise mobility ecosystem which drives solution approaches.

6.1 Mobile First

Mobile first is an approach which emphasizes on design philosophy for mobile applications or even complete solution approach. There was a time where the mobile was considered as just an extension to the current working system. It was considered as good to possess kinds of offerings. In such an approach, applications or solutions were designed as web portal or desktop executable in mind where some limited features as per priority were extended on mobile for end users.

With proliferating space, mobile has taken over user's major time and focus on day-to-day activities. Even more mobiles are sold than the number of babies born in a day. It occupies personal as well as professional life.

The mobile-first design philosophy emphasizes on mobile perspective. It is recommended to start designing and thinking for small screen first, then move towards bigger screens. Consider a scenario where a complete solution is designed with mobile perspective, where important workflow with user preferences for the system, user's behaviour, and interaction-model with heterogeneous mobile platforms are analyzed first. On the basis of study result, respective solution approach is designed. Here, design considers mobile UI/UX flow, interactions, behaviour, responsiveness, performance, and application overall designs. User delightful experience can be achieved with consideration of certain parameters like grid-based visual layouts, visual designs, ratio-based responsive designs, calculated chromes, and contrast ratios. Mobile applications can be designed in two approaches as adaptive design and app-centric design.

Mobile first has introduced several benefits and opportunities to explore untapped territories. Significant betterment on ROI can be observed after adoption of mobile-first philosophy.

6.1.1 Adaptive Design

This design approach emphasizes more on platform-specific guidelines over application design. Here application flow, UI components, and interactions models are designed as per platform guidelines. Mobile platforms (Android, iOS, Windows Phone, and other) possess their own design guidelines and recommendations. In this approach, the same application may look distinct with platform-specific mobile devices. It also requires consideration of diverse form factors, screen resolutions (smartphone, tablet, and phablet), and even different OS version specific guidelines (if any).

6.1.2 App-Centric Design

This design approach emphasizes on application branding and flow. It is not driven as per mobile platform-specific guidelines. In this approach, mobile application looks the same on all mobile platforms though it also requires consideration of diverse form factors, screen resolutions (smartphone, tablet, and phablet), and common factors on different platform-specific guidelines. This design philosophy gives uniqueness to application objective with branding.

Note

Adaptive design and app-centric design are standard approaches for mobile application design irrespective of mobile first.

• •

6.2 Gamification

Gamification is the process for objective user engagement. It has more to do with psychology and less with the technology. It requires thorough understanding of target-user segments' psychology, their work habits, motivations factors, work schedules, etc. It brings the engagement attributes of games on enterprise systems to drive a positive change in the behaviour of users. It helps to motivate and engage the workforce in the processes and be more productive. It is not about transformation of the work into a game, but it is about identification of new ways to engage users with progress visibility, performance metrics, instant feedback, rewards, and acknowledgement. Gamification process emphasizes on three major aspects as points, badges, and leaderboards, which is also known as PBL system.

[I.] Points: These are the numbers given to any task or flows to end users in solution approach, which brings statistical comparison parameters among different users.

[II.] Badges: These are the labels or recognition to users for their job or task achievement.

[III.] Leaderboards: It is a space which emphasizes on number statistics, recognitions, highest achiever, ranking, etc. It is shared among the target user community and visible to complete user segment. This can be designed via distinctive infographical charts.

Other important perspectives for the gamification process are motivation factors, rewards, and mission where motivation factors can be studied as per user psychology and introduced as points, badges, or leaderboard stats. Mission provides specific details about their work objective with points statistics. Rewards can be redeemed after achieving a certain defined level.

Gamification requires understanding of user psychology and defining a complete solution with target as user engagement with the system. This results as user productivity, which in turn can provide betterment on ROI to enterprises.

6.2.1 Gamification Steps

This overall gamification approach requires target user segment study (psychology, behaviours, etc.) and accordingly design of game rules for the ecosystem. The following are the phases and steps for gamification approach implementation with enterprise mobility solutions.

[I.]   Identification Phase:
    a) Identify the target user and study user psychology
    b) Define the success criteria or objective of overall solution
    c) Work on motivation factors, mission, and rewards

[II.]   Design Phase:
    a) Define perfectly challenged levels which should not be too simple/complex
    b) Keep the game rules simple, define PBL
    c) Keep the leaderboard small, with well-defined user's social network and peers in the group
    d) Design the mobile app
    e) Gamification elements should be merged with the design

[III.]   Execution Phase:
    a) Identify required mobile platforms
    b) Selection within hybrid versus native versus web mobile app
    c) Implement gamification rules as designed

[IV.]   Measure and reiterate

6.3 Wearable Devices

Earlier, the mobile was used for audio calling and text messaging. It was not feasible to imaging mobile usage for personal and professional work, though over time mobile has emerged as an opportunity for personal and professional work–life management.

Wearable devices may repeat history. Proliferating and emerging wearable devices are at experimental state for various domains, sectors, and segments. The following are some of the feasible wearable devices with focus on usability perspective:

[I.]   Clothes (shirt/trouser): Conductive-thread manufactured clothes can power and communicate with other wearable devices.

[II.]   Shoes: Integrated sensors and GPS (Global Positioning System) with shoes can be used for generating power with movement, health monitoring, tracking kids or people, navigation to destination, etc.

[III.]   Glasses: Internet-connected glasses with computing power can be utilized for important notifications, navigation with distance and direction, Internet browsing, over the voice command, music player, radio, audio/video call, camera picture, audio/video recording, etc.

[IV.]   Wristband/Bracelet: Integrated sensors with wristbands/bracelets can be used for health monitoring (body movement, sleeping habits, etc.), communication with other gadgets, notifications/ alerts, etc.

[V.]   Ring: Personalized ring with storage/computing power can be used as identity proof and store valuable details, like passport, license, credit card details, etc.

[VI.]   Wristwatch: Integration of computing power and storage capability can make wristwatches as mini mobiles with versatile features, like vibrate on messages/notifications, send and receive voice calls, install and use apps, monitor health, use as a storage device, work as camera for pictures and audio/video recording, make dinner reservation, etc.

[VII.]   There can be many other wearable devices (earrings, necklaces, belts, etc.).

For the consumer market, wearable devices (smartwatch, wristband, glasses, etc.) can be a part of luxury lifestyle. Either, they can also be an opportunity, if designed and marketed attractively. Here, the mobile can be a good example.

The following are some of the feasible cases for wearable devices:

[I.]   Health Sector: Wristband for patients at hospital, giving alarm to doctors' (cabin/mobile) in case of health issues, which are measured through various sensors.

[II.]   E-commerce: Wristwatches for customers with a payment feature. This wearable device can verify user identity and process payment via vendor devices.

[III.]   Access Authentication: Wearable devices (wristband, bracelet, ring, wristwatch, etc.) can be used as an identity-proof asset while entering the office gate or an authentic place. It can display user's personal details on gate glass/monitor, and gate would open only for authorized persons.

[IV.]   There can be many other similar cases.

For enterprises, business objective association is mandatory for any entity to be a part of the enterprise ecosystem. Mobile offering contributes to enterprises in the form of increased and efficient productivity. Similarly, if wearable devices use case can be accommodated to the enterprise ecosystem with measurable ROI, then soon it can be a part of the enterprise radar.

6.4 Hybrid

In the horizon of enterprise mobility, hybrid (amalgamation of thoughtful, respective, best-of-breed technology) emerged as the preferred approach whether it's about server hosting or mobile app development. Hybrid is the approach considered for reducing TCO.

Any enterprise solution that requires server hosting infrastructure and available options can be on-premise, cloud, or hybrid (as discussed in earlier sections). Hybrid hosting infrastructure considers both cloud and on-premise and uses the best of their offerings as per enterprise solution designs. Private cloud, public cloud, or a combination of both is also feasible as per enterprise objectives, which in turn helps to achieve adequate infrastructure cost, security, and measurable ROI.

Availability of diverse mobile platforms is one of the challenges for any enterprise application. Cross-platform support is the imperative expectation for any mobile application. Along with cross-platform support, it is also expected to cover platform-specific diverse form factors by mobile applications. Such kind of diversity among mobile devices and technology resulted in hybrid to be a preferred implementation approach. Below is the figure to illustrate hybrid versus native on a scale of time and cost.

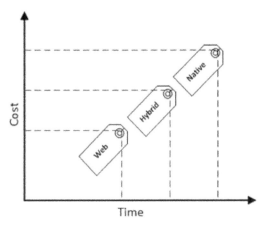

Figure 6-1: Hybrid

Note

Hybrid versus native mobile application is a debatable topic. Experts have counter opinions and recommendations across various forums.

6.5 IOT

IOT phrase, which stands for Internet of things, is an umbrella consisting of uniquely identifiable network-connected embedded devices, supported communication protocols, relevant technologies, and server components. These network-connected embedded devices are often connected with sensors or data gathering systems like Internet-connected cars, wearable devices, smartphones, etc. These IOT devices with or without UI are basically used for collecting and processing the data of everyday usage.

6.5.1 Classification

Broadly IOT can be classified in three layers consisting of server components, communication gateway, and devices. The figure below illustrates classification in three layers.

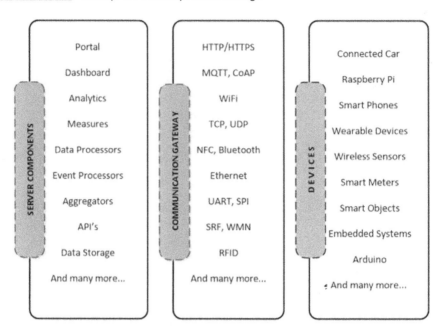

Figure 6-2: IOT Layer Classification

Server components are required for assorted analytics, measures, processing, and storage by system. Communication channels are identified and designed as per device and solution expectations. Some of the communication protocols are MQTT (message queuing telemetry transport), CoAP (constrained application protocol), NFC (near field communication), UART (universal asynchronous receiver transmitter), SPI (serial peripheral interface), SRF (shaped radio frequency signal), WMN (wireless mesh network), RFID (radio frequency identification), etc.

IOT devices are also identified and designed as per solution statement. Some of the devices are Raspberry Pi (small size single-board computer), smart object (an object with own possible interactions), wireless sensors, embedded systems, connected cars, etc.

IOT solution or system expects attention to cater respective challenges associated with devices, like:

[I.]   identity and access control

[II.]   security of private data (secure credentials and other personal data)

[III.] authenticated channel of communication

[IV.]   automatic updates (data wipe, data backup, suspend/resume, enable/disable features, preferred communication networks and settings, etc.)

[V.]   remote management (monitor, locate, and block device)

[VI.]   limited power, memory, and processing capability

[VII.] device risk management (handle reverse engineering and other attacks)

6.5.2 Applications

Proliferating and emerging IOT applications can be integrated with any domain, sector, or business statements. The following are some of the IOT applications:

[I.]   Home/hotel or building automation with various sensors and managed by single device. For example, home appliances (refrigerator, TV, AC, washing machine, lighting, etc.) are managed by mobile phone

[II.]   Health monitoring automated systems via sensors and communication to relevant devices

[III.] Real-time communication among driver, vehicle, traffic, and other entities in transport systems

[IV.]   Electronic devices automation and management over the air for effective usage of power or energy

[V.]   Enterprise departments process optimization via automated sensors. For example supply chain management process optimization while manufacturing, transporting, etc.

[VI.]   Monitoring and controlling of various bridges, railway tracks, hospitals, etc. for infrastructure management via IOT devices

[VII.]   Emergency services automation with sensors to track environmental factors as earthquake, storm, etc.

[VIII.]   Monitoring and analysis of wildlife movements for required management and wildlife security

[IX.]   Tracking and analysis of user likes and locations for smart shopping solution

SUMMING UP

✓   Mobile first is a design philosophy with recommendation to design solutions with mobile perspective. It suggests to design and implement mobile solutions as per target platforms, UI/UX guidelines, and user expectations. However, traditional approach for mobile application was to leverage mobile as an extension with limited feature of existing working web or desktop solution.

✓   Mobile applications can be designed with two approaches as adaptive design and app-centric design.

✓   Gamification is the process of psychological study of the system and implementation of identified game elements with required technologies to achieve the goal of user engagement.

✓   Gamification basic elements are points, badges, and leaderboards (PBL).

✓   Wearable devices are growing fast for the consumer market but yet to explore their ways to entertain enterprise system.

✓   Hybrid has emerged as the preferred approach for enterprises, either it's for hosting or mobile app development.

✓   IOT is an acronym used for uniquely identifiable network-connected embedded devices with communication protocols, technologies, and server components.

✓   Some of the IOT devices are connected cars, Raspberry Pi, smartphones, wearable devices, wireless sensors, smart meters, smart objects, embedded systems, Arduino, etc.

ACTION ITEMS

- ✓ What are the Gartner predictions for IOT?
- ✓ What are your opinions on hybrid approaches for enterprise? Also check popular forums and expert recommendations.
- ✓ Identify effective usage for wearable devices at enterprise ecosystem.
- ✓ Is gamification applicable only for mobile solutions?
- ✓ Identify and list down the differences between adaptive design and app-centric design for mobile applications.
- ✓ What is Internet of everything?

7. CASE STUDY

KEY POINTS COVERED

- ❖ · Case Study on Enterprise Mobility Solution
- ❖ Enterprise Needs and Challenges
- ❖ Solution Overview

7.1 Introduction

XYZ is a consumer electronics manufacturer enterprise situated in USA across diverse geographies. The enterprise deals in manufacturing of electronics and sells through several distributor showrooms to consumers. Their principal USPs are product quality and service to consumers which help them to be a differentiator in the competing market.

XYZInfotech is an IT company with focus on enterprise mobility end-to-end solutions. Being SI, it harnesses expertise and experience for strategizing and implementing enterprise mobility solutions. The company is the technology partner to XYZ enterprise and worked on end-to-end solutions.

Note

This case study is a hypothetical scenario for understanding. If it matches with any real product/service/solution from respective enterprise/ company/organization, then it would be just a coincidence.
••

7.2 Challenges

The enterprise is able to manage product quality via well-defined managed and controlled quality standards. However, they are facing challenges in services to consumers for product installation, repair, maintenance, and customer complaint though they possess basic infrastructure in place with FSEs (field service engineer). FSEs have expertise and experience in electronic products service, and they report to the ASM (area service manager), who takes care of FSEs schedule and task management. But their current way of handling customer complaint requires several manual interventions at a distinct level which causes delay to serve end users. The enterprise is looking for generic solutions with mobile offerings for system users. It is expected to serve consumer motives with optimized and efficient ways to improve on service quality, hence customer satisfaction.

7.3 Solution

As per enterprise mobility maturity model, XYZ enterprise grades at level one with support of email, IM, and the imperative mobile apps for product marketing. They also possess fine-grained and well-defined policies for their IT infrastructure support. These are implemented and maintained by XYZInfotech. XYZ is an enterprise looking for measurable ROI for each penny either in the form of money, workforce efficiency, productivity, or increased sales/marketing. The enterprise is not reckoning for big infrastructure setup at on-premise hosting though security is always a concern. So XYZInfotech has provided adequate solutions and setup as per their need with cloud-hosted web services infrastructure and mobile apps hosted at platform-specific app stores. The enterprise is not keen to possess EAS as their objective can be achieved with platform-specific consumer app stores as Google Play, Windows Marketplace, and Apple Store, considering the enterprise's major mobile user base at Android, WP, and iOS.

7.3.1 XYZ-Artemis

One of the enterprise's objectives is to harness a common solution across all service centres. XYZ-Artemis is the solution designed and implemented by XYZInfotech to cater field service and other enterprise objectives. The figure below exemplifies system users and their workflow.

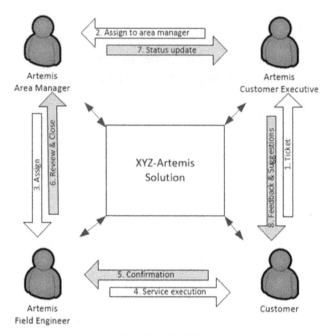

Figure 7-1: Artemis Flow

Identified users for Artemis solution are:

[I.] Customer: One who has requested for the product service, either for installation, repair, etc.

[II.] Customer Executive: Point of contact for customer. He/she verifies customer ticket request, collect feedback, and suggestions after request completion.

[III.] Area Manager: He/she owns area-specific enterprise customer service responsibilities, manages field engineers for task allocation and status review, and facilitates them for customers' request effective execution.

[IV.] Field Engineer: Product engineer for field service at customer location. Reports to area manager.

[V.] Management Executive: Enterprise management representative for analyzing respective performance and execution status and reports.

[VI.] Administrator: Supreme user of the system for assorted settings, customization, access rights, branding, etc.

7.3.2 Use Cases

Here are the cases for system users with features that they can use or perform.

7.3.2.1 Customer

Customers of Artemis can perform the following actions:

[I.]   sign up and sign in
[II.]   log ticket(s)
[III.]   track ticket(s)
[IV.]   update ticket(s)
[V.]   sign out.

7.3.2.2 Customer Executive

Customer executives can use the following features from Artemis system:

[I.]   sign in
[II.]   view ticket(s)
[III.]   update ticket(s)
[IV.]   assign ticket(s)
[V.]   sign out.

7.3.2.3 Area Manager

The Artemis system allows the following features to be used by the area manager:

[I.]   sign in
[II.]   view report(s)
[III.]   view ticket(s)
[IV.]   log ticket(s)
[V.]   assign ticket(s)
[VI.]   update ticket(s)
[VII.]   close ticket(s)

[VIII.]   sign out.

7.3.2.4 Field Engineer

Field engineers can use the following features of the Artemis system:

[I.]   sign in
[II.]   view ticket(s)
[III.]   ticket map view
[IV.]   ticket check-in
[V.]   update ticket(s)
[VI.]   ticket check-out
[VII.]   sign out.

7.3.2.5 Management Executive

Below are the features to be used by the management executive:

[I.]   sign in
[II.]   view report(s)
[III.]   sign out.

7.3.2.6 Administrator

The Artemis system allows the following actions to be done by the administrator of the system:

[I.]   sign in
[II.]   add staff member(s)
[III.]   customize ticket fields
[IV.]   settings
[V.]   customize branding
[VI.]   customize report options
[VII.]   manage access rights
[VIII.]   sign out.

7.3.3 Architecture

XYZ-Artemis is the solution designed as per enterprise objective. It considers scalability and manageability parameters for future solution extensions. Hence, its components are implemented as pluggable independent modules. Below is the figure which exemplifies several participating entities and components for the Artemis solution.

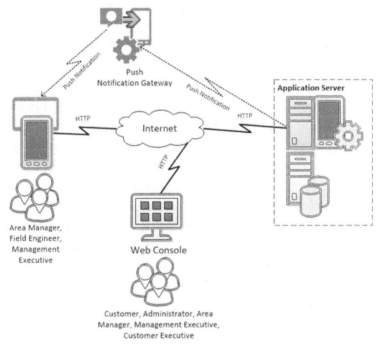

Figure 7-2: Artemis Architecture

XYZ-Artemis architecture consists of the following pluggable modules:

[I.]   Push Notification Gateway: It is based on open-source third-party server-side library PushSharp for push notification support on diverse mobile platforms as Android, iOS, and WP.

[II.]   Application Server: It is implemented with SOA design approach based on J2EE frameworks. This component of the system takes care of business logic, database CRUD, operation, and exposes required RESTful web services.

[III.]   Mobile Application: It is a mobile hybrid application based on Apache Cordova platform. The application supports Android, iOS, and WP on tablets and smartphones. It is designed for the area manager, field engineer, and management executive with role-based application access and flow. Mobile applications are deployed over Apple Store, Google Play, and Windows Store.

[IV.]   Web Console: AngularJS-, HTML-, and CSS-based web application using RESTful web services for data communication. It is designed and implemented for customer, area manager, customer executive, management executive, and administrator with role-based application access and flow.

[V.]   RESTful Web Services: Communication among distinctive modules or components has been designed and implemented with RESTful web services, which transfers encrypted data to client applications.

7.5.4 Summary

Artemis solution has been designed and implemented for mobile aware enterprise (enterprise mobility maturity model—level 1) with scalability and manageability considerations. It is able to achieve the enterprise target for effective and efficient field service for customers. MDM/MAM were out of scope for this solution as data is not very critical for enterprise, though basic level of security has been implemented for data over communication and data at rest. A mobile application has been implemented with hybrid approach because that reduced TCO. Users were asked to bring their own device for mobile application usage. Web console usage has introduced the necessity of desktop systems for administrator, customer executive, area manager, and management executive. Customers' flow (sign up, sign in, and ticket access) has been integrated with the enterprise's web side. Basic level of modifications and enhancements has been supported by administrator console to cater to immediate system needs.

Appendix A: Services, Products, and Solutions

Enterprise mobility is a wide and rapidly emerging field. Every few months, there are major value additions by vendors, service providers, manufacturers, and products. Enterprise mobility offers services, products, and solutions.

[I.]   Services: These are well-defined managed services to perform certain objectives of enterprise mobility. They are managed services with amalgamation of business objective and technical backbone.

[II.]   Products: These products can be customizable, off-the-shelf vertical or horizontal products to cater to specific features under enterprise mobility—for example MAM product which is ready to integrate with enterprise applications.

[III.] Solutions: These are thoughtful combinations or integration of services, products, tools, frameworks, and platforms to achieve enterprise-grade applications. Generally solutions can be customized and assembled out of pluggable independent modules or components as per enterprise objective.

There are many organizations/companies working on products, solutions, or services with focused approach to be a differentiator among the market, and they market and sell their products, solutions, or services.

There are companies which work as system integrators where they are not implementing or manufacturing anything. However, they possess expertise and experience on integrating distinctive products, services, and solutions for end-to-end enterprise mobility solutions. SI (system integrators) role is a challenging work with such a wide variety of solutions, services, and distinctive products available in marketplace. They may do marketing and selling for their area of specialization with emphasis on domain expertise. This even helps enterprises to identify appropriate SI as per desired objective.

Appendix B: Food for Thought

Enterprise mobility is comprised of various business objectives, solutions, products, services, frameworks, tools, platforms, and many more. It is obvious to have certain things which are debatable among the forums, communities, and groups.

[I.] Native versus hybrid mobile application is one of the topics of debate among forums, communities, and groups. Basic features and details about native, web, or hybrid mobile applications have been covered under technology and trend section. Some prefer native applications due to its responsiveness, user interactions, and luxuries to use device capability at high extent. However, hybrid gets priority for cross-platform development support, cost, and time efficient development cycle. Selection among hybrid or native app totally depends on the lineaments of an application because both possess their own pros and cons. For example, if an enterprise focuses upon leveraging a wide variety of device platform users and early market approach, then hybrid can be a good option. However, if a company has more stress on application performance and user interactions, where cost and time-to-market is on second priority, then native application is the right choice. Though, with well-designed and implemented hybrid application, performance can be near to native application. And native-like application can also be implemented with hybrid frameworks or tools.

[II.] EMM is one of the buzzwords with forums, communities, and groups. It is not a point for debate.

But it is the field which is getting emerged. There are many queries and concerns with EMM—for example, difference within enterprise mobility and EMM features which comes under EMM suites.

[III.]   Understanding enterprise mobility is like swimming in an ocean of acronyms and abbreviations. Many technical and marketing acronyms and abbreviations have been traversed in seven sections of this book. However, this is not the end of the list. There are many more such acronyms and abbreviations—for example, enterprise collaboration platforms, EAM (enterprise asset management), EAM (enterprise architecture management), EAI (enterprise application integration), EMM (enterprise marketing management), EII (enterprise information integration), EI (enterprise integration), and many more.

Rıx: Best Practices

It is challenging to bind enterprise mobility with technologies, solutions, platforms, frameworks, and domains. And it is complex to define guidelines for unbounded surface, though there are some best practices or approaches which can be considered while working for any enterprise mobile solution. Below are the Rix (R Nine) best practices for pathway to enterprise mobility.

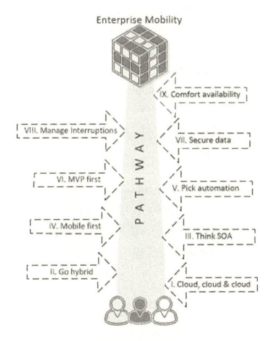

Rix: Best Practices

[I.]   Cloud, cloud, and cloud

Infrastructure setup is the big bottleneck for enterprise mobility solutions and one of the major concerns from enterprises. Cloud computing has revolutionized the way of software application implementation and infrastructure support. Proliferating cloud computing can be married with growing enterprise mobility. Together they can serve the imperative objectives of enterprise for scalability, extensibility, and flexibility. Enterprises can leverage their own private cloud or host their services on public cloud. Enterprise mobility solutions can also opt for already existing SAAS-based EMM solutions. Enterprise mobility with cloud will be the driver in the future for enterprises.

[II.]   **Go hybrid**

Enterprise adoption over BYOD introduces diverse mobile platforms, devices, and form factors to be covered while mobile application is being developed. Hybrid is the cost-effective and rapid development approach for mobile applications. They can be managed and scaled due to platform independent codebase approach. Improved and enhanced mobile technology stack allows feature-rich hybrid mobile application development. It is recommended to go hybrid until it is not compulsory to implement native mobile application due to any business or technical reason.

Hybrid mobile applications are the amalgamation of respective technologies, frameworks, tools, and platforms. Hence, solution architecture, design, and development approach plays pivotal role for mobile application UI/UX and responsiveness.

[III.]   **Think SOA**

Service-oriented architecture facilitates scalability, extensibility, manageability, and robustness to the solution. It is recommended to design and implement a solution with SOA thoughtfulness. For cloud-based mobile applications, SOA is a rescuer for rapid developments and enhancements.

[IV.] Mobile First

Application user interaction and design are the important factors for success of any application. Application ease of use and intuitiveness are the primary factors as per application UI/UX. And mobile is an unavoidable part of enterprise solutions due to its huge adoption over the society. It is recommended for enterprise solutions to go with mobile first. This requires thinking first on small screens. Hence, mobile application and solution are designed and implemented for small screen, afterwards followed by desired bigger screens. Application UI/UX can be designed with application-centric or adaptive designs. However, it is recommended to consider platform-specific guidelines while designing.

This approach is also important for overall solution architecture perspective. In general, solutions are designed and implemented for full-featured web/desktop client; subsequently mobile client applications are extended. This may introduce some architectural limitations at mobile client application in the form of screen design, user interaction, application performance, etc.

[V.] Pick automation

Any task or exercise which requires repetitive execution is an opportunity for automation. At first look, automation may be a consumption of time and money. However, in the long run, it facilitates extensibility, scalability, and flexibility to the solution.

Under the horizon of enterprise mobility, feature-rich application demands performance analysis and validation of mobile application to verify device CPU, network, memory, battery consumption, application responsiveness, etc. It is challenging and time-consuming to perform manual testing and verification on diverse mobile platform devices and form factors for diversified geographies, networks, and languages. Test automation tools can be a saviour to overcome manual testing of these myriad options of platforms, devices, form factors, geographies, networks, etc.

[VI.]   **MVP First**

MVP stands for minimum viable product. It is always a point of concern for enterprises to prototype first version of solution with adequate features and investments. MVP first approach is important to cater versatile mobile domain. It may not be worth it to invest time and money for full-featured application at first release. It is recommended to design and implement MVP for first release of application. This helps on budget control and management. Solution can be designed with integrated analytics tools for users' behaviours. And further application and solution releases can be done as per users' real-time behaviours, feedbacks, and suggestions which are extremely required for success of any application.

[VII.]   **Secure data**

Enterprise data security is one of the primary concerns from CIOs and an important factor for solution design and development. Enterprise application solutions should consider proper security mechanism and respective handling. It would consider data on the move as well as data on rest at device. Secure enterprise gateway can be implemented as per enterprise manoeuvre with adequate firewall, secure network communication, preferred network, etc. This would also require well-defined policies to enforce with enterprise users. EMM suite solutions can be considered for security enforcement at devices.

Data storage on device can be avoided till it is not required. Stored data can also be made secure with storage at application secure sandbox in encrypted format. Memory management at mobile application is also an important perspective for data storage and security. It is recommended to induce micro level of memory management for enterprise application. This would help to avoid any unwanted data storage while the application is in session as well as when application is offline. Mobile platforms also provide programming guidelines for memory management, and it is expected to be followed for enterprise mobile applications.

[VIII.] **Manage interruptions**

There are many interruptions for mobile applications which demand to be managed gracefully for enterprise-grade mobile applications—for example, low battery, network availability, application suspension/resumption, incoming call, text message, push notification, etc. An enterprise mobile application is expected to manage all such interruptions. They are important for data security and application usage. Mobile platforms also provide programming guidelines for interrupted handling, and they should be followed while application is being developed—for example, proper memory object cleaning and state management with low battery notification, thread safe process execution, images/audios or other resources released while application is suspended. Application state and graceful interruption management is required to avoid premature exit of enterprise application.

[I.] **Comfort availability**

Enterprise mobile application availability and distribution is the final outcome of all exercises. This plays a pivotal role for the success of a solution. Hence, it has to be planned while designing the solution. There are various consumer application stores (Apple Store, Google Play, Windows Phone Store, etc.). Application-distribution strategy depends on the type of application. For consumer applications, it can be planned with consumer application stores. However, for enterprise users, it has to be planned accordingly. Applications can also be embedded with devices before their launch in the market by having an alliance with renowned device manufacturers, like Samsung, Apple, Nokia, etc.

The enterprise has to identify and plan as per device environment (BYOD, CYOD, or COPE) and the corresponding integration of EMM suite solutions (EAS, MAM, or MDM). In general, users may not agree for MDM solution on personal devices though MAM solutions can be planned if the enterprise opted for BYOD or CYOD. MDM solutions can be planned with COPE where the enterprise applications can be preloaded with devices. Even the device customization can be done as per enterprise objective. Renowned application stores (Apple Store, Windows Phone Store, etc.) also facilitate enterprise-grade application distribution features. These can also be explored while designing a solution.

References

'Android (operating system)', *Wikipedia, the free encyclopaedia* <http://en.wikipedia.org/wiki/Android_(operating_system)> accessed 12 July 2014.

'AngularJS', *AngularJS* <https://angularjs.org/> accessed 15 August 2014

'AngularJS', *Wikipedia, the free encyclopaedia* <http://en.wikipedia.org/wiki/AngularJS> accessed 15 August 2014.

'Apache Cordova', *Apache Cordova* <http://cordova.apache.org/> accessed 15 August 2014.

'Apple push notification service', *Apple* <https://developer.apple.com/library/ios/documentation/NetworkingInternet/Conceptual/RemoteNotificationsPG/Chapters/ApplePushService.html> accessed 30 September 2014.

'Apple Store', *Apple* <http://store.apple.com/us> accessed 30 September 2014.

'Arduino', *Wikipedia, the free encyclopaedia* <http://en.wikipedia.org/wiki/Arduino> accessed 20 July 2014.

'BlackBerry', *Wikipedia, the free encyclopaedia* <http://en.wikipedia.org/wiki/BlackBerry> accessed 15 July 2014.

'Bootstrap', *Bootstrap* <http://getbootstrap.com/> accessed 14 August 2014.

'C2DM', *Google* <https://developers.google.com/android/c2dm/> accessed 28 September 2014.

'CCXML', *W3C* <http://www.w3.org/TR/ccxml/> accessed 20 November 2014.

'Constrained Application Protocol', *Wikipedia, the free encyclopaedia* <http://en.wikipedia.org/wiki/Constrained_Application_Protocol> accessed 15 June 2014.

'Cocoa', *Wikipedia, the free encyclopaedia* <http://en.wikipedia. org/wiki/Cocoa_(API)> accessed 18 June 2014.

'Dual tone multi frequency signalling', *Wikipedia, the free encyclopaedia* <http://en.wikipedia.org/wiki/Dual-tone_ multi-frequency_signaling> accessed 20 July 2014.

'Embedded System', *Wikipedia, the free encyclopaedia* <http:// en.wikipedia.org/wiki/Embedded_system> accessed 20 August 2014.

'Enterprise mobility management', *Wikipedia, the free encyclopaedia* <http://en.wikipedia.org/wiki/Enterprise_ mobility_management> accessed 18 May 2014.

'GCM', *Android* <https://developer.android.com/google/gcm/ index.html> accessed 30 September 2014.

'GRXML', *W3C* <http://www.w3.org/TR/speech-grammar/> accessed 20 November 2014.

'Google Play', *Google* <https://play.google.com/store?hl=en> accessed 21 May 2014.

'iOS', *Wikipedia, the free encyclopaedia* <http://en.wikipedia.org/ wiki/IOS> accessed 12 July 2014.

'Internet of things', *Wikipedia, the free encyclopaedia* <http:// en.wikipedia.org/wiki/Internet_of_Things> accessed 15 December 2014.

'iPad', *Wikipedia, the free encyclopaedia* <http://en.wikipedia. org/wiki/IPad> accessed 15 July 2014.

'iPAQ', *Wikipedia, the free encyclopaedia* <http://en.wikipedia. org/wiki/IPAQ> accessed 15 July 2014.

'Interactive voice response', *Wikipedia, the free encyclopaedia* <http://en.wikipedia.org/wiki/Interactive_voice_ response> accessed 20 November 2014.

'JavaEE', *Oracle* <http://www.oracle.com/technetwork/java/ javaee/overview/index.html> accessed 15 June 2014.

'jQuery', *jQuery* <http://jquery.com/> accessed 14 August 2014.

'jQuery Mobile', *jQuery mobile* <http://jquerymobile.com/> accessed 14 August 2014.

'LESS', *{less}* <http://lesscss.org/> accessed 15 August 2014.

'Mobile enterprise application platform', *Wikipedia, the free encyclopaedia* <http://en.wikipedia.org/wiki/Mobile_enterprise_application_platform> accessed 24 May 2014.

'MQTT', *Wikipedia, the free encyclopaedia* <http://en.wikipedia.org/wiki/MQTT> accessed 21 November 2014.

'Model view controller', *Wikipedia, the free encyclopaedia* <http://en.wikipedia.org/wiki/Model%E2%80%93view%E2%80%93controller> accessed 21 June 2014.

'Model View ViewModel', *Wikipedia, the free encyclopaedia* <http://en.wikipedia.org/wiki/Model_View_ViewModel> accessed 21 June 2014.

'Nokia', *Wikipedia, the free encyclopaedia* <http://en.wikipedia.org/wiki/Nokia> accessed 12 July 2014.

'Personal digital assistant', *Wikipedia, the free encyclopaedia* <http://en.wikipedia.org/wiki/Personal_digital_assistant> accessed 20 July 2014.

'PushSharp', *PushSharp Github* <https://github.com/Redth/PushSharp> accessed 19 September 2014.

'Raspberry Pi', *Wikipedia, the free encyclopaedia* <http://en.wikipedia.org/wiki/Raspberry_Pi, http://www.raspberrypi.org/> accessed 21 August 2014.

'Representational state transfer', *Wikipedia, the free encyclopaedia* <http://en.wikipedia.org/wiki/Representational_state_transfer> accessed 15 June 2014.

'Radio-frequency identification', *Wikipedia, the free encyclopaedia* <http://en.wikipedia.org/wiki/Radio-frequency_identification> accessed 22 November 2014.

'Singleton pattern', *Wikipedia, the free encyclopaedia* <http://en.wikipedia.org/wiki/Singleton_pattern> accessed 15 June 2014.

'Smart objects', *Wikipedia, the free encyclopaedia* <http://en.wikipedia.org/wiki/Smart_objects> accessed 10 November 2014.

'Service-oriented architecture', *Wikipedia, the free encyclopaedia* <http://en.wikipedia.org/wiki/Service-oriented_architecture> accessed 01 December 2014.

'Serial peripheral interface bus', *Wikipedia, the free encyclopaedia* <http://en.wikipedia.org/wiki/Serial_Peripheral_Interface_Bus> accessed 19 September 2014.

'Single sign-on', *Wikipedia, the free encyclopaedia* <http://en.wikipedia.org/wiki/Single_sign-on> accessed 03 November 2014.

'Symbian', *Wikipedia, the free encyclopaedia* <http://en.wikipedia.org/wiki/Symbian> accessed 02 July 2014.

'Universal asynchronous receiver/transmitter', *Wikipedia, the free encyclopaedia* <http://en.wikipedia.org/wiki/Universal_asynchronous_receiver/transmitter> accessed 19 November 2014.

'VXML', *W3C* <http://www.w3.org/TR/voicexml30/> accessed 20 November 2014.

'Windows Phone', *Wikipedia, the free encyclopaedia* <http://en.wikipedia.org/wiki/Windows_Phone> accessed 12 July 2014.

'Windows Phone Store', *Windows phone* <http://www.windowsphone.com/en-in/store> accessed 12 July 2014.

'Wireless mesh network', *Wikipedia, the free encyclopaedia* <http://en.wikipedia.org/wiki/Wireless_mesh_network> accessed 15 November 2014.

'Windows push notification services', *Microsoft Windows* <http://msdn.microsoft.com/en-in/library/windows/apps/hh913756.aspx> accessed 15 September 2014.

INDEX

'It is a splendid and spectacular book. A must-read for all enterprise mobility practitioners.'
—Ilirijan Residovski (co-founder and business analyst at SOLOMO Technology Inc., Madison, USA)

'Unless you have been hiding under a rock for the last few years, it is impossible to not be aware of the growth in mobile technology. Raghvendra's book is a no-nonsense practical guide that can help any business to first understand and then develop a strategy to best take advantage of the opportunities of an enterprise mobility breakthrough.'
—Andrew Leach (entrepreneur, Darlington, UK)

'Really great, very readable, and eminently useful enterprise mobility book. It prominently clarifies enterprise mobility subtleties.'
—Kishor Kumar Singh (senior technical lead, India)

www.ingramcontent.com/pod-product-compliance
Lightning Source LLC
Chambersburg PA
CBHW051247050326
40689CB00007B/1101